Notes on Contributors

William J. Bryans, FCIS, FHSM, is area administrator for the Southern Health & Social Services Board, Co. Armagh, Northern Ireland, and has a special responsibility for management and organisational development.

Isobel Curry, OBE, RGN, is estate development manager for the North West Thames Regional Health Authority, London.

Averil Dongworth, MBA, DN(Lond), RGN, is unit general manager at the Luton and Dunstable Hospital–Acute Services.

Suzanne Goodband, SRN, RSCN, RCNT, DN(Lond), is manager of children's services, Riverside Health Authority, London.

Christine Hancock, SRN, BSc(Econ), is general secretary of the Royal College of Nursing.

Gordon Hemsley, BA(Econ), MIPM, is district personnel manager, Parkside Health Authority, London.

Penny Humphris, BA, MSc(Econ), AHSM, is managing consultant with the Health Care Group, Peat, Marwick, McLintock.

Tom Keighley, RGN, RMN, NDNCert, RNT, DN(Lond), BA(Hons), is director of nursing for the Waltham Forest Health Authority, Essex.

Dr Alison Kitson, DPhil, BSc(Hons), RGN, is RCN standards of care director and head, research and evaluation, Institute of Nursing, Radcliffe Infirmary, Oxford.

Laurie McMahon, BSc, MSc, is fellow in management & organisational development at the King's Fund College, London.

Josephine Plant, BSc, RGN, RM, is chief nursing officer and director of service quality, Lewisham & North Southwark Health Authority, London.

Trevor Ride, BA(Hons), RGN, RMN, IHSM(Inter), is assistant to the general secretary, Royal College of Nursing.

Jolyon Vickers, RSCN, RGN, ONC, Dip. in Health Information Service, is district information officer with Maidstone Health Authority, Kent.

Contents

Acknowledgements

Many individuals have contributed to this book, some of them unwittingly. The case study material has been drawn from a variety of sources, based in the experience of the contributors and as a result of contact and discussion with a wide range of health service workers and clients. We are indebted to all of them and would like to record our thanks.

Preface

This book is intended to help those who have recently taken up managerial positions in health care. There is no shortage of books and articles which describe and analyse managerial roles in the National Health Service, but few of them are addressed more specifically to the newly appointed manager. As the title suggests, this volume is targetted at health professionals, and nurses in particular, who have made the move to general management, but its messages are equally applicable to new general managers from other backgrounds.

In the past twenty years, nurses, as managers, have come of age. Following the Salmon reorganisation, assistant matrons became 'nursing officers', shedding the purely administrative chores and taking up both clinical and managerial responsibilities. Their sphere of influence, however, was limited to nurses and nursing, and the potential of these nursing 'hybrids' was never fully realised, largely because of a lack of credibility as clinicians with their professional peers, and as real managers with health care administrators.

Changes within the nursing profession have enabled those nurses who wish to remain in practice to have a much longer clinical career 'at the bedside'. At the same time, the Griffiths reorganisation has considerably expanded the range of opportunities for nurses who are keen to assume wider managerial reponsibilities. Their functional background has prepared them well for this task and we believe that the experience and skills of ward sisters and community nurses will provide a fertile seedbed for the first line general managers of the future. Managers with a nursing background are ideally placed to regulate, coordinate and monitor the use of resources and to assess the outcomes of care.

In designing this book, our purpose was to expose the reader to problems and issues that are likely to face most general managers. We felt that this could best be achieved by presenting each issue through a case study, which is then analysed and resolved, and from which some general conclusions are drawn. We also felt that, wherever possible, it would be appropriate to select authors who are practising managers and who are able to present the issues with a realistic flavour that comes from years of battle-scarred experience! This is, therefore, a practical book rather than an academic tome. We hope that it will be used by the manager, puzzling over the way to resolve some thorny managerial problem, who is seeking some fresh inspiration. At the point when he or she says, 'I wish I could talk to someone who has been through this problem', we hope that our manager will turn to the appropriate chapter for that helpful insight from an experienced manager which will provide the key to resolve the problem.

Management is not a neat or tidy business. While students may learn about information systems, budgeting or capital planning as nicely discrete subjects, the reality is that the boundaries between topics are ill-defined. This book has also been divided into apparently well-defined chapters, but readers will find that, as in reality, the subject matter of the chapters naturally overlap. We have arranged the chapters in three groups: the first group (Chapters 1–3) examines what might be called the macro-management issues of planning health care, developing a management structure and managing people. Within the context of these wider issues the second group (Chapters 4–11) looks at the more technical matters that face the general manager, while the final chapter considers how – with the body of knowledge and technical skills that the manager possesses – he or she can develop an approach which will make changes happen. It is not without significance that the final words of this book are 'common sense'.

The reader will probably not wish to read the book from beginning to end. Each chapter stands on its own – a resource to be used whenever the reader feels in need of 'external advice'. There is, however, a general pattern that runs through most of the chapters: a brief introduction, a case study followed by an analysis of the problems and solutions, concluding with some general principles. Many of the chapters use case studies with a nursing flavour, so that readers coming from a nursing background will feel familiar with the context of the case study. This should not, though, deter readers from other backgrounds, who will be able to apply the ideas even though the territory may not be their natural habitat.

We should like to extend a warm thanks to the contributors to this book who not only agreed to write on the subject that we requested, but also accepted that they should, in general terms, conform to the format that runs through the book. It is not easy to write within a pre-determined template, and the twelve authors have shown extraordinary patience with us.

Pauline Fielding
Philip C. Berman
1990

1
Planning Health Care
Christine Hancock

1.1 Introduction

Planning is the process of suggesting how the future could be different from the present; which changes are necessary, and how these changes should be brought about. Planning health care is as complex as is the notion of health itself. Health is the product of so many influences: genetic characteristics, the environment, wealth or poverty, employment or the lack of it, personal behaviour, and last of all medical care. Health care planning, in its widest sense, is concerned with all these factors and with the social and economic policies that give rise to them. In a more limited way, the policies and development of health services can, and should be, directly planned both by people working in those services and by those who use them or may use them in the future. Planning in a bureaucratic health service often seems to be the art of writing a plan, though it should in fact be the art of achieving change.

A model of planning should consider:

- What is the problem to be addressed?
- What is the planning intended to achieve?
- What form should planning take?
- How is the planning to happen?
- What are the outcomes of planning?

Planning for the health needs of elderly people will illustrate most of the issues which have to be addressed in the overall planning of health services.

1

1.2   What is the problem to be addressed?

Planning needs to consider both the national and the local context. Since the second world war, the proportion of elderly people in Britain has been steadily rising: in 1951 11 per cent of the people in Great Britain were aged over 65 and now there are 15 per cent. Retirement leads to people adopting different lifestyles, due to changes in their daily routine and usually due to a fall in income. The personal health of people in their sixties, however, shows little change from their earlier years. It is in their seventies that increasing disability leads to more complex demands on medical and social services. Of people aged 65 and over in local authority residential accommodation, more than 80 per cent are aged over 75, and indeed 40 per cent are over 85 years old.

In Woodlands, a hypothetical health district chosen to illustrate the planning of health care, it is possible not only to know the total population or that aged over 65 and over 75, but it is also possible to know this for very small areas which have, in this case, a population each of between 6000 and 12000 people. The characteristics of these small areas are available from the national census which is published every ten years and will enable the planners to recognise that the proportion of people aged over 65 varies from 13 per cent to 24 per cent across the district and that the proportion of them living alone varies from 4 per cent to 8 per cent.

These general figures can be supplemented by more detailed and more specific information as well as less quantified and more anecdotal information from the professionals working throughout the district. Information such as census data is very specific and easy to interpret; however, as a full census occurs only every ten years, the data can be very out of date.

Other information, such as that from health care workers, will also be useful but may be difficult to quantify in a way which enables comparisons both over time and between health authorities. For instance, across the country there is an eightfold variation in the numbers of elderly people treated by home nurses. Home nursing provision is highest outside London and especially in the non Metropolitan counties where it is some 90 per cent greater than it is in Inner London. Information clearly has to be more than just about numbers of elderly people.

In Woodlands, predictions show a diminishing number of people aged over 65 but a rapid increase in the proportion aged over 75 (some 7 per cent); a predicted increase in the number of elderly people from black and ethnic minority groups, and an increase in elderly people who are married, as opposed to the current position where single and widowed people are the great majority. All this information should inform plans for the future provision of health care for elderly people.

An audit is necessary to assess the capability of the present service:

● Where are the differences with similar districts?
● Where are the problems and difficulties?

Each year since 1983/4, the Department of Health has issued a set of performance indicators (PIs) on computer disks to each English health authority. These comprise a collection of proportions, ratios and indices which are particularly useful to managers and which identify how a district or specialty fares on a set of PIs in relation to the rest of the country. PIs permit comparisons with national and regional averages and identify districts which lie in the top or bottom 10 per cent on any indicator (Figure 1.1). Recent PI packages allow time series analysis so that changes in performance over time can be analysed (Figure 1.2). PIs should, however, be used with caution and sensitivity as local variations in conditions can mean that like is not compared with like; they are indicators of performance, not measures.

Figure 1.1 PIs for Elderly Services in Woodlands Health Authority. Compared with other health authorities, the district's services for elderly people are satisfactory.

	DHA value	Eng. min.	middle 80 per cent of England values are between ‹›	Eng. max.
Institutional care rate–hospital	7.50	.700		20.4
District nurse contact rate	24.7	6.10		68.1
Day patient attendance rate–geriatric	492.0	0		2081
First admission rate–Elderly MI	0.7	0		13.2

Figure 1.2   Institutional care rate for the elderly

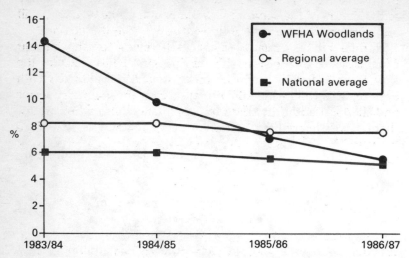

PIs are merely the starting point for suggesting areas which require further investigation and should be used in a spirit of enquiry, not one of inquisition. PIs are most effectively used by peers reviewing service issues and performance by comparing local performance with that of colleagues elsewhere. Used in this way, PIs can help spread good practice.

Clearly an analysis of the health service resources available to the client group is most important. However, this may be complicated: not all elderly people will be cared for in beds designated for the aged. Some old people will appropriately be treated in surgical and psychiatric inpatient facilities; the vast majority will receive their health care from their general practitioner; much care will be provided by other agencies, and reports have shown that many old people have needs which are not being addressed at all.

Traditionally, planners find it easier to measure service provision by tangible measures such as beds and day places. It is much harder to identify the total financial resources being spent on elderly people given the way in which health service budgeting is undertaken at the moment. Rarely is enough attention given to the people who actually provide the service. Every old person, most of their families, and many health care workers themselves, recognise that the major difference in the quality and quantity of the service provided is due to the number, skill and approach of the staff employed to work in that service.

A final but essential element to a review of the current capabilities of any local health service must be to consider the service provided by agencies other than the National Heath Service. This will include the private sector, the voluntary sector and the local authority. Elderly people and those who care for them have the right to expect a service which is seam-free between the various provider agencies; regretfully this is rarely the case.

1.3   Case study

An age-related hospital service for elderly people was set up in Woodlands Health Authority to provide acute medical care when needed. Despite a reduction in the allocation of funds over the years 1982–4 the health authority increased the number of district general hospital beds available for elderly patients and improved home nursing services. The outcome of the changes made were assessed against the aims of the service by using data from the Hospital Activity Analysis, SH3 returns, government population estimates, and yearly figures collected locally. By introducing an age-related service in one health authority, people aged over 65 were seen to have benefited.

1.3.1   Background

Before 1983 the health service provided to elderly people in the district was very traditional. There were 404 beds (49 on the district general hospital site) and fewer than 900 deaths and discharges a year. The waiting list for admission fluctuated between 40 and 60 people waiting at home for a bed and similar numbers awaiting transfer from other specialties.

1.3.2   Objectives

In 1980 it was proposed to develop a service to:

1. Make more beds available at the district general hospital for

the immediate admission of elderly patients with acute medical problems.

2. Eliminate waiting lists.
3. Persuade doctors and other professional staff of the needs of elderly people for acute medical care.
4. Discharge elderly people when the benefits of being in hospital ceased.
5. Reduce the demand for institutionalised residential care.
6. Relieve the pressure on short stay medical beds.

An age-related service was defined as that in which any person who required non-surgical acute admission and who was aged 75 or over would be admitted to the department for elderly people. As for admission to other specialties, the initial assessment is carried out in the accident and emergency department before a patient is transferred to the ward; there is no catchment area restriction for acute cases. Because of the relatively small number of district general hospital beds for elderly people there is a system of 'progressive patient care', whereby people who require longer hospital stays are transferred to beds on other hospital sites. If the district general hospital beds are full, the people aged 75 and over are admitted to general medical beds, and likewise if these beds are full, younger patients are admitted to the department for elderly people. There is no age criterion for non-acute referrals from general practitioners and other consultants.

This type of service was preferred to an integrated service for the following reasons:

1. The combined consequences of morbidity and social deprivation are met with increasing frequency with age. The needs of younger elderly people (aged 65 to 74) for hospital services are similar to those of other younger people, but those aged 75 and over are more likely to have specific problems owing to their age.
2. There were low expectations, little enthusiasm, and a sense of hopelessness concerning the care of elderly people. Offering to relieve the general medical services of the workload of elderly people would encourage the more reluctant physicians to transfer resources as well.

3. The health authority had 2.8 acute beds per 1000 population and was under great pressure to reduce this number. The redesignation of medical beds to beds for elderly people helped lower the number of short stay beds while retaining the number of beds on the district general hospital site that were available for acute cases.
4. The increase in the number of people aged 75 and over and the decrease in the number of those aged 65 to 74 focused attention on the need to put specialised services where they are most needed.
5. If an integrated service had been introduced, specialist skills would have been spread over 11 wards at the district general hospital, rather than five, and it would have been difficult to introduce and sustain a high quality of care.
6. Age 75 was the lowest age that could be chosen because of workload.

To achieve the required reductions in revenue, the district health authority closed first a ward of 20 beds at an outlying hospital, then a convalescent home (26 beds) and another hospital (58 beds) – a net reduction of 104 beds for elderly people, none of which were on a district general hospital site. This was offset by a reprovision of 58 beds, 25 on the district general hospital site, and an increase of £50000 for district nursing services. In addition, 49 general medical beds at the district general hospital were redesignated as beds for elderly people. Thus there was an increase of 73 beds on the district general hospital site, resulting in a total of 122 (29 per cent of all beds for elderly people). These figures are from SH3 data for 1982 and 1984 and from the Office of Population Censuses and Surveys population estimates.

1.3.3 Results

The number of deaths and discharges from all beds rose from 948 in 1980 to 3282 in 1984. This increase was entirely due to the throughput in beds on the district general hospital site – that is, the average number of deaths and discharges per available bed each year – where deaths and discharges rose from 380 in 1980 to 2853 in 1984. Of these 2853 discharges, 70 per cent were discharged home, 8 per cent required transfer to a non-district general hospital bed, 3 per cent were transferred to another speciality, and 19 per cent died during the initial admission.

The number of people aged 75 and over per 1000 catchment who were admitted to a non-surgical district general hospital bed increased by 70 per cent from 91 in 1980 to 155 in 1984. The improved access, however, was limited to district general hospital beds. Length of stay was reduced to 12.6 days and turnover interval to 2.2 days, with an increased bed occupancy of 85 per cent and throughput of 24.7 people per bed a year by 1984.

The occupancy of non-district general hospital beds fell from 93 per cent in 1980 to 81 per cent in 1984. This suggests that there is less need for residential care in hospital, though the following may have contributed:

1. The local authority introduced a home care programme which enabled more severely physically disabled people, considered to be too disabled for Part III homes, to live at home rather than in hospital;
2. The number of places in private and voluntary homes increased from 97 in 1981 to 164 in 1985.

By 1983 there was no longer a waiting list for admission from the community. This was achieved before the increase in district general hospital beds. Since 1984 there has been no delay in the transfer from other specialties of elderly people who live in the catchment area and would benefit from medical services as shown by the census data collected yearly in January (Table 1.1).

Table 1.1　One-day census of numbers of people in general medical beds age 65–74 and 75 and over who were in hospital for over eight weeks and over 12 weeks in 1983, 1984 and 1985.

	1983		1984		1985	
Weeks (no.)	*over 8*	*over 12*	*over 8*	*over 12*	*over 8*	*over 12*
Aged 65–74	13	0	10	2	13	1
Aged 75 and over	22	4	5	1	5	0

Table 1.2 Costs and savings (in parentheses) of developing services for elderly people in Woodlands Health Authority 1982–4. (Figures are rounded to the nearest £1000 and are at 1983 prices.)

	£000	
Closure of hospital	(1100)	
Closure of convalescent home	(120)	
Closure of non-district general hospital ward	(150)	
Total	(1370)	(1370)
Redesignate 49 general medical beds to 49 beds for elderly people on district general hospital site	155	
Reprovide 25 beds on district general hospital site from hospital closure	303	
Additional costs of reproviding 33 beds on non-district general hospital site	55	
Increase district nursing services	50	
Increase nurse staffing to existing district general hospital beds	58	
Increase nurse staffing to non-district general hospital beds	70	
Increasing medical staffing levels	48	
Total	739	739
Total saving	(631)	

There are no data on readmission rates and there are considerable difficulties in measuring and interpreting these. From one small survey it was concluded that 11 per cent of patients discharged were readmitted within one month, but the reason for the readmission was not assessed.

The savings from introducing the service were £631 000 at 1983 prices (Table 1.2). Of these, £412 000 came from the change of use of general medical beds and £219 000 from closing beds for elderly people. These savings were realised even after the increases in nursing and medical staff. In addition, the convalescent home was sold for £375 000 and the hospital site for £30 million in 1988.

The numbers of deaths and discharges of people aged 75 and over for all acute non-surgical beds increased by 89 per cent after an age-related service had been introduced. This increase was probably due to a combination of previously undetected medical needs which are now being met. Effective hospital care is now being provided for a greater number of apparent 'social problems', whose illness while treatable had not been recognised – because of the historical high dependence on accident and emergency departments rather than on primary health care services.

Before 1983, despite improvements in medical staffing, an age-related admission policy and a good rehabilitation service, there was only minimal improvement in performance. Only when a critical number of beds was achieved on the district general hospital site was a better service offered to elderly people.

Over 95 per cent of elderly people live in their own homes, some relying on services from statutory and non-statutory agencies. Community services support profoundly disabled people but cannot manage patients with acute illness. The district general hospital services recognise and respect the special needs of elderly people (an essential community resource), without which community care falters and fails.

1.4 What is the planning intended to achieve?

The audit of the current services should lead to a definition of the purpose of planning. It is then necessary for all concerned in the organisation to agree what the planning is intended to achieve. A plan that has value will need to incorporate the shared views and goals of all those with a stake in the eventual service; the 'stakeholders' will be:

● Elderly people themselves
● Those who will become elderly during the planning period
● Their families, friends and other informal carers
● The staff of the health service, both professionals and others
● The local authority
● Key local voluntary organisations

A statement of philosophy might be as follows:

The local health authority exists to provide a service; that service should arise from the needs of the community and reflect the most efficient and effective use of the resources available. That service should also be non-discriminatory in access, and constantly changing to meet changing priorities. Decisions about the health service should be taken in such a way as to maximise public and staff involvement. Those who receive health care should be the principal evaluators of the service.

The ideas expressed in such a statement of philosophy are very simple and, if all concerned are equally committed to them, then both planning and implementation may also be simple. However, this is rarely the case! From a statement of purpose or philosophy such as this it should be possible to agree some principles of planning:

● Home is the best place for an elderly person to receive care.
● The person in need should determine what service is required
● Staff are important
● The relationship of staff to those who receive health care is one of service
● The service which is planned has to be that which can be afforded

1.5 What form should planning take?

From such statements of philosophy and principles of planning the health authority can set goals for its plans which should be understood and shared by staff working in the health service. The goals of the Woodlands plan for services for elderly people were agreed as being:

● To enable people to make their own decisions about their health
● To care for people at home and outside institutions whenever possible
● To establish a partnership between the health service and other groups to provide care for elderly people

● To provide health care for elderly people on a local basis
● To provide health services that are efficient and effective
● To develop plans which are amenable to evaluation, prefer-
  ably on a continuous basis
● To offer accessible and equitable health care for elderly people
  in terms of geography, ethnicity and gender

It is often difficult for the health service to be clear about 'what
business we are in' but in Woodlands it was agreed that the
primary responsibilities were three:

● To promote health and prevent ill health
● To treat ill health by primary health care and in hospitals
● To provide residential care for people with severe disabilities
  caused by physical, psychological and social problems

Locally, Woodlands decided it had a central role and ownership of the first two of these responsibilities. The authority
recognised its contribution to residential care (and had over the
past few years improved the standard of that residential care
quite substantially) but felt that it was not an essential part of its
business. Rather it was something the health service had in-
herited historically but which was probably better done by other
agencies (housing and social services, private and voluntary
sectors).

1.6   How is the planning to happen?

Planning meetings sound (and often are!) the most boring of
health service activities. It is essential that the process of
planning is such as to encourage and not hinder the participation of clinical staff. It is they who bring to the planning process
a proper understanding of the present pattern of service and an
interpretation of future plans realised into new practices.

Planning needs to take account of those who understand the
planning processes, especially of the health service, but also of
local government and the voluntary sector; of those who practice
in the specialty; and of those who have a stake in the plans for
the future. It is essential therefore that the language used is easy

to understand so that it encourages and does not inhibit that participation. The clinical staff have a particular responsibility to describe issues in ways which help planners and statisticians to do the research, investigation, and analysis which is necessary. Meetings of planning groups can be arranged in different ways:

1. At regular intervals with carefully prepared papers distributed well in advance so that everyone can read them properly.
2. In unstructured brain storming sessions to exchange ideas and visions of the future.

It is often helpful if a small number of a large planning group meet between the formal meetings in order to progress the work of the full group.

Planning groups need to consult and seek advice throughout the planning process. This can be done by seeking written views, by talking to those with a known interest, by sharing widely documents which are at an early stage of discussion.

1.7 What are the outcomes of planning?

Despite the priorities outlined earlier, local services for elderly people were actually addressed first and most spectacularly by a revolution of the acute medical services. That was in part because the dynamic leadership came from a young consultant physician. She recognised that the district had too many beds and that most of the beds were in the wrong places.

A rapid move to a direct age-related admissions policy enabled the appropriate skills of highly trained consultant physicians and their supporting staff to be brought to the early assessment and diagnosis of the presenting illness of all people aged over 75. The skills of the team specialising in the care of the elderly people included a high standard of acute medical diagnosis and treatment, specialised nursing and intensive rehabilitation. The team recognised the multiplicity of factors which often combine to produce a medical crisis in an elderly person and the need to ensure the coordination of the appropriate social and environmental factors in order to ensure recovery and return home.

After five years of this approach there was a significant reduction in the requirement for long stay residential care. This provided the opportunity to invest in community and preventive services in order to support elderly people discharged rapidly from the acute hospitals, thus preventing an early readmission for the same condition.

1.8   Problems and solutions

Planning the services which elderly people will require from a district health authority is a model for the whole process of planning. Elderly people make demands on every part of the health service with the exception of those services designed specifically for children or pregnant women. Some aspects of planning for elderly people are more reliable than for other groups; for example, population projections and forecasts are notoriously inaccurate, but have the highest level of accuracy for elderly people, all of whom are already born!

Probably the greatest weakness of the approach described was that insufficient consideration was given to the need to secure commitment from a broad spectrum of people. As a result, a great deal of time was spent, after the changed policy had been implemented, in providing explanation and understanding to a wide range of people including social services staff, local authority members, and even community nurses. What happened showed, in many ways, that a small number of entrepreneurial people can achieve real and rapid change in the health service, but that they need to secure wide understanding and support of that change in order for the greatest benefit to be realised.

Several areas still require attention and investment while continuing the important momentum and change which has already occurred. The work that still needs to be done is in the area of health promotion and appropriate residential care for those elderly people who will not be able to manage at home.

As part of the planning process, a positive approach to health in old age needs to be promoted in order to shape the attitudes and actions of many people both in and outside the NHS. Good health is a precious resource, at least for elderly people. Mortality

Table 1.3 Life expectancy at age 65

	Males			Females		
Circa	1900	1950	1980s	1900	1950	1980s
Australia	11.3	12.2	14.3 (83)	12.9	14.4	18.6
Belgium	10.6	12.3	12.9 (79)	11.6	13.9	16.9
Canada	—	13.3	14.5 (82)	—	15.0	18.7
Ireland	10.8	12.1	12.5 (81)	10.6	13.3	15.8
Japan	10.1	11.2	15.7 (84)	11.4	13.2	19.3
Netherlands	11.6	14.1	14.0 (83)	12.3	14.7	19.0
New Zealand	12.2	12.9	13.6 (83)	13.3	14.8	17.5
Norway	13.5	14.9	14.5 (83)	14.4	16.0	18.7
Switzerland	10.1	12.4	15.5 (84)	10.7	14.0	19.8
England & Wales	10.8	12.0	13.1 (82)	12.0	14.4	17.2
United States	11.5	12.7	14.6 (82)	12.2	15.0	19.1

Sources:
Demographic Yearbook 1957, 1983 (New York: United Nations, 1957, 1985).
World Health Statistics Annual 1983, 1984, 1985 (Geneva: World Health Organisation, 1983, 1984, 1985).
Economic Survey of Europe in 1974. Part II, Post War Demographic Trends in Europe and the Outlook Until the Year 2000 (New York: United Nations, 1975).

rates among older people have been falling and most people believe that health or morbidity is improving. The improvements that have been achieved in recent years are certainly impressive, though the performance of other nations demonstrates that we can do more (Table 1.3).

'Old age' is not acceptable as a diagnosis for ill health, and the view is spreading that the pathology of later life can be treated, often cured, and in many cases can be better managed. One objective would be to raise the general standard of health, a second to reduce the prevalence and severity of common illnesses and health problems. Planning needs to consider improvements in the health of today's elderly people as well as the best possible health for elderly people in the future. The health of the country's elderly people will be enhanced by improvements in nutrition, housing and higher personal expenditure on home heating, as well as by a decline in smoking and excessive alcohol consumption and by attention to exercise. It would also be improved if drugs and medicine were more selectively prescribed, instructions adhered to and follow up assessments and clinical reviews undertaken.

More and more information is available about what constitutes good physical and mental health. The dissemination of such information to elderly people at local level should be a vital part of the planning process; this would make it possible to enhance self care, increase active involvement in decision making, and enable individuals to have a greater impact on future service provision and on policy making.

Self care in the elderly population is important in another sense. The majority of elderly people are retired, but also active, fit and energetic. From their number are found not only many of the family carers of other elderly people, but also a huge potential resource for disseminating advice and practical help. It is often difficult for remote bureaucratic organisations like health authorities to identify all the voluntary groups that are now helping with transport, shopping or home maintenance, and thought is only now being given to finding effective ways of encouraging the mutual and spontaneous support and care among elderly people. Community staff can be vital both in promoting self help initiatives and in providing information on community based projects.

Community care in practice very often means care by families and relatives (normally wives or daughters) caring for older people. Many carers require support and relief at critical stages in order to fulfil their obligations. Yet it is common practice for a health authority to withhold or even withdraw its services if a female carer is present. When assistance is sought from the health service, plans need to be made to ensure that support is not only forthcoming, but that it is flexible and geared to providing relief to carers.

1.9   Some general principles

Statements of philosophy and principles, and the setting of clear goals as part of the planning process, will enable the health authority and its staff to set objectives. These need to be concerned both with the promotion of health and an approach to the prevention of illness as well as with plans to deliver health care that genuinely recognise the needs of local people. Planning requires an analysis of local health services in order to ensure that the service is provided as close as possible to people's own homes and makes the best use of the resources available. Since a service plan has to be afforded within the resources available, a budgetary framework must be developed which matches spending patterns with service priorities. Planning health care also requires the health authority to provide for the development and training of its staff in a manner which recognises their full potential.

There are a number of ways in which planning can be approached:

1.9.1　Rational approach

The rational approach involves the assessment of need, followed by the development of a whole range of options before a comprehensive plan is produced.

1.9.2　The incremental approach

The incremental approach suggests that planning has to be based on limited information, and that the uncertainty of the future makes small decisions preferable to grand plans. Planning is, in fact, often a legitimation of actions taken – often in stealth – either by NHS staff or by voluntary organisations or pressure groups.

1.9.3　The political approach

The political approach recognises that planning is a response to various pressures and constraints from government, professions, pressure groups and others.

In practice, planning is usually a compromise of all three. Traditionally, planning has been singled out as a special kind of management activity all on its own. It is seen as being about the future, of trying to predict what the future may hold, and then attempting to prepare for the likeliest contingencies. As such, it is often seen as something different from management, which is more concerned with immediate pressures, difficulties and opportunities, all of which have to be addressed in what is often a very short timescale.

Strategic planning pulls together philosophy, structures, principles and assumptions into a coherent planning response to the organisation's need. It assumes that this task can be undertaken:

● Systematically, in identifying the different responses, their characteristics and resources
● Evaluatively, in assessing choices
● Developmentally, in building on experience and skills which allow more effective responses in the future

It is important to realise, however, that none of the planning theories provides clear guidelines for practice. Planning as a concept has assumed a substance and tangibility in the National Health Service which the present state of the art does not warrant. On the contrary, it is essential to ask basic questions about the influence that planning may have on organisations. Planning for the redistribution or decline of a service is critically different from planning which is based on the expectation of growth. The concept of planning is one in which success depends in part on the clarity of the strategic direction.

The use of formal planning systems as a means of controlling expenditure and performance of one level of the organisation by another will result in a different emphasis from that produced by the use of planning systems to develop change within a local health organisation.

This case study has shown that information and diagnosis are essential but not enough; that leadership and champions of the idea are also essential but not enough. What is also essential is to have widespread understanding and shared ownership of plans as they evolve and are implemented. The best plans may die for want of the appropriate level and skills of staff to work within a developing service. Plans must include the plans and ideas of other statutory organisations, of voluntary organisations, of informal carers and the users of the service themselves. The health service still has a long way to go to evolve ways of bringing all those views together with equal weight.

A pattern of major objectives, purposes or goals and essential policies and plans for achieving such goals has to be stated in a way which defines 'what business' one part of the health service is in and how it wants to 'do business'.

Planning does not arise merely from the reflections of top managers. There is an upward flow of values and opportunities and of perspectives on issues and problems, which substantially help to form the plan for an organisation. Such an approach to planning makes strategy a structuring force in any organisation which defines the relevant problems and how and by whom they are to be tackled.

1.10 Sources of help and information

Planning for health care is a complex business and it is something which has to be shared and worked at together by a number of managers and professionals. Plans exist in all health authorities and a good start is always to read plans of previous years, plans of neighbouring districts and plans of the region. Publications from government departments, professional bodies and the various independent institutions all provide a point at which to start the process of planning. The approach described here draws on a number of sources of help and information:

1. Quantitative information

● World Health Organisation statistics, WHO Regional Office for Europe, Scherfigsvej 8, DK – 2100, Copenhagen, Denmark
● Office of Population Censuses and Surveys statistics, OPCS, St Catherine's House, 10 Kingsway, London W2B 6JP
● Small census information from OPCS
● DoH Performance Indicators
● Operational Research Service, 151 Great Titchfield Street, London W1P 8AD

2. Audit of local service

● Facilities, staff, finance
● Professional practice and standards
● Views of staff and users

3. Ideas of good practice:

● Consumers and voluntary organisations
● Professional books and journals
● Staff in the service

Bibliography

'Benefits of effective hospital services for elderly people', *British Medical Journal* (17 October 1987)
Community Care Developments (National Audit Office, 1987).
Improving care of elderly people in hospital (London: Royal College of Nursing, 1987).
OPCS Population Trends No. 45 (London: OPCS, 1985).
The promotion of health among elderly people (London: King's Fund Institute, 1987).

2
Developing a Management Structure
Penny Humphris

2.1 Introduction

Many managers will, at some time in their careers, need to develop a management structure. All managers will, several times in their careers, need to consider whether an existing structure is the most effective way of organising the service for which they are responsible. This chapter uses a case study to illustrate the process of introducing a new management structure and draws from it a framework which can be used in any part of an organisation as an approach to developing or reviewing a management structure. Finally, the general principles to be observed in developing a management structure are summarised.

2.2 Case study

The introduction of general management in the NHS led to the appointment of general managers at unit level during 1985 and 1986. This case study describes the experience of a unit general manager (UGM) appointed to a large provincial teaching unit with over 1100 beds, 4000 staff and a revenue budget of £42 million, with the opportunity of introducing a management structure without any posts or roles being prescribed.

The existing management structure was based on functional management with each profession managing itself and very limited management input by consultants. This had led to slow decision making, inflexible resource use, excessive professionalisation, a lack of personal accountability and the absence of a single person with overall responsibility for the organisation. The UGM needed to refocus management on the main business of the organisation and to involve consultants in decision making.

2.2.1   The beginning

The first task was to meet and talk with as many staff as possible, in order to understand the business of the unit. As major changes to the management arrangements were likely, the UGM recognised that there was a high level of anxiety among nurse managers, administrators and department heads, all of whom felt vulnerable and threatened. It became important that early progress was made in publishing proposals to try to minimise uncertainty.

One dilemma the UGM faced was how to progress ideas about future management arrangements to ensure the best ideas within the organisation were incorporated, but to avoid confusion about the precise nature of the arrangements. On balance, the UGM decided to share ideas about the future at initial meetings with senior staff and when visiting wards and departments, in order to obtain preliminary feedback. Unfortunately, as the ideas grew and took shape through discussion, they changed in many aspects, so the emphasis when talking to the thirtieth person was different from that at the outset. This led to some doubt, rumour and confusion, yet the alternative approach would have been to circulate written proposals for consultation without any prior discussion.

In addition, although the UGM had a vision of how the management of the unit should be in three to five years' time, careful thought had to be given to how much knowledge of future change the organisation could cope with at one time. The ideal was to create a climate in which senior staff felt themselves to be part of evolution rather than revolution.

2.2.2   The business of the organisation

Discussion revealed that most staff believed the organisation existed to provide the best possible services to patients. The district health authority's strategic and annual operational plans described objectives in terms of care or client groups and supporting services. The government required district health authorities to provide services within cash limited financial allocations. All these gave clues in reaching the conclusion that the focus of management had to be the delivery of services to patients or care groups.

The existing functional management arrangements, in which nurses managed nurses, administrators managed hotel and administrative services and the doctors had no role in the management process, were clearly unsatisfactory. Instead, a more appropriate grouping of activities for management purposes would be the creation of a management structure based on cohesive and logical areas of clinical activity. So, for example, child health would be defined as a clinical service with one person managing as many as practicable of the resources used in providing services to children.

Consideration of the clinical activities of the unit and how these could best be grouped into services raised a range of issues to be resolved. These included:

● Sense of identity
● Specialty or sub-specialty
● Span of control

The unit consisted of two main hospitals – one of about 850 beds with a range of specialties and one of about 250 beds for obstetrics and gynaecology. The larger hospital did not provide staff with any sense of belonging because of its size and the functional management structure, so the creation of defined clinical services would give staff a sense of identity. The small hospital already gave this sense of belonging to its staff and it was important to develop management arrangements which allowed this to be retained.

The various possible ways of dividing the total clinical activity had to be considered. Should there be one service for surgery or should separate services be established for urology, ear, nose and throat surgery, maxillo-facial surgery? Should cardiology and cardiac surgery be together, or divided to join medicine and surgery respectively? Should trauma and orthopaedics be linked with accident and emergency services? How should service specialties such as radiology and pathology be included?

The answers to these questions, and many like them, gradually emerged from discussion with staff and consideration of the nature of the activity, geographical location and degree of interaction between the services involved.

Some were obvious. For example, a link was logical between ear, nose and throat and maxillo-facial surgery since they shared two wards. Cardiology, cardiac surgery and thoracic surgery shared a ward floor and were regionally funded, so logically formed a clinical service in their own right. Others were more tricky. For example, should the cardio-thoracic intensive care unit be linked with the general intensive care unit to which it stood adjacent sharing the necessary nursing expertise, or with the cardiothoracic service of which it was a crucial part? In such dilemmas, a decision had to be made, but with sufficient flexibility built into the management structure to allow the services to interrelate.

It is generally accepted that the maximum number of subordinates who can be adequately supervised by one manager is about eight to ten. If there are more than this, it may be necessary to create additional layers of management to exercise effective control.

Finally, after long deliberation, the UGM identified 13 clinical services as the focus for the management structure (Figure 2.1).

Figure 2.1 The clinical services

Accident and emergency
Anaesthetics/intensive care/theatres
Cardiology, cardiac and thoracic surgery
Child health
Ear, nose and throat and maxillo-facial surgery
General medicine, rheumatology and rehabilitation
General surgery and urology
Geriatric medicine
Neurology and neurosurgery
Obstetrics and gynaecology
Pathology
Radiology
Trauma and orthopaedics

2.2.3 *Decision-making in the clinical services*

The UGM then considered the types of decisions which had to be made in the clinical services. A clear distinction was required between management decisions and decisions involving clinical judgement.

Management decisions made in the services would be concerned with:

- Providing the highest quality and widest range of services within the total resources available
- Finding ways of maximising and making the most effective use of the total resource

Clinical decisions would be concerned with:

- The treatment which is offered or given to an individual patient by his doctor

It would therefore be quite inappropriate for any manager to interfere in clinical matters which are the very essence of the doctor–patient relationship.

However, given current methods of NHS funding, in which a financial allocation unrelated to workload is made to regional and district health authorities and thence to units, and given the infinite demand for health care, decisions had to be made about how the resources should be used. Since a large number of such decisions were and would continue to be made at the clinical level by consultant medical staff, the UGM considered it essential to involve them in the management process. However, consultants are appointed because of their clinical expertise and do not necessarily have the inclination, the time or indeed the skills to become deeply involved in management. The UGM recognised their contribution needed to be in providing leadership and overall clinical direction and so determined that each service should have a consultant as the clinical service director.

Adequate provision had then to be made for the full time management of each clinical service to complement the leadership and direction which would be provided by the clinical service directors. The UGM therefore decided to appoint for each clinical service a manager who would be responsible for the day to day running of the services, managing nursing, clerical, secretarial and appropriate professional and technical staff, and the budgets for junior medical staff, drugs, dressings, medical and surgical supplies and equipment, printing and stationery, and so on. In time it was hoped that information systems could be established to allow the clinical services to 'buy' theatre time, pathology and radiology services.

2.2.4   Supporting services

Each clinical service would depend on a range of non-clinical supporting services including domestic, portering, catering, laundry, sterile services, works. Since it was impracticable to divide the management of these between the 13 clinical services, and as most required specialised management, the UGM established a structure in which the managers of supporting services reported through a senior manager, the site services manager, to the UGM. Emphasis was placed on encouraging the managers of both support and clinical services to recognise the nature of their relationship, namely that clinical service managers are consumers of support services on behalf of patients and that support service managers are providers of service in support of the delivery of patient care.

2.2.5   Staff functions

Having decided to focus the management arrangements for the unit on clinical services, the UGM had to decide which staff functions were required to provide advice and service to line managers. Creating satisfactory lines of communication between line and staff managers is one of the most difficult problems of organisations, as managers of staff functions are often extremely experienced but have no managerial authority over the line managers.

Given the size of the unit's financial allocation, financial advice and support would be needed by all operational managers who would have budgetary responsibilities. In addition, the UGM required central control and monitoring of the total allocation. Consequently, a financial management section was established, headed by an accountant as the unit's finance manager, to provide financial advice and support to both the UGM and all operational managers.

Over 4000 staff were employed, so the UGM regarded the availability of personnel advice and support as essential for all operational managers. A personnel section was established, headed by a personnel manager, to provide a full range of personnel advice and services.

As the Unit needed to be able to respond to changing health care needs and priorities and to develop strategic plans for each clinical service, a planning manager was appointed to lead this activity, involving the clinical service directors and managers.

2.2.6   Requirements for professional advice

The introduction of general management to the NHS inevitably created tensions among the professions, many of whom had emerged over the past 40 years with their own management hierarchies after prolonged struggles for recognition. As the UGM planned to cut through professional structures in focusing general management on clinical services, mechanisms had to be established within the unit for obtaining professional advice and ensuring that its benefits were not lost.

Medical advice would be obtained from the clinical management board consisting of the 13 consultants who were directors of clinical services, the unit general manager and a representative of the faculty of medicine. To obtain nursing advice, the UGM established the senior management post of patient care manager to provide a focus for the nurses in the unit and to give professional advice to the UGM, directors and managers on issues of clinical practice, education and conduct. In order that the post holder should, in his or her own career interests, have some line management experience, responsibility was attached to the post for certain support service departments. Other senior managers, such as the finance and personnel managers, would provide professional advice relating to their individual spheres of responsibility as well as contributing to the overall management of the unit.

2.2.7   Consultation

Having determined the shape of the management structure, the

UGM addressed the question of how to begin the process of consultation and implementation. Moving from one management structure to another in a large and busy unit would not be easy. The UGM decided that a paper setting out the proposed structure should be widely circulated and comment invited. During the eight weeks given for consultation, the UGM spoke to many groups of staff, outlining the proposals, answering questions and receiving comment. A large number of responses was received, some totally supportive, others totally condemnatory. A number of practical points were raised, so the UGM decided to incorporate responses to these in a final version of the management arrangements.

A major issue was the type of professional background the managers of clinical services needed. The UGM strongly believed it was general management skills or potential which were essential, rather than a body of specialist knowledge, and that the posts should be available to people from any professional background. The nursing profession felt equally strongly that posts with management responsibility at this level should be filled only by nurses because of the responsibility for direct patient care services and the fact that a large number of staff managed would be nurses. Considerable unease was expressed because all nursing management and administrative posts would disappear, to be replaced by general management posts with responsibility for specific clinical services. To avoid prolonged uncertainty, arrangements for filling the posts by internal competition were announced as early as possible in the implementation process.

2.2.8   Implementation

Four months after the consultation document had been circulated, the final version of the management arrangements, including outline job descriptions for the posts, was issued. The organisational structure is shown in Fig 2.2. Implementation began almost immediately. Clinical service directors were either nominated by their consultant colleagues or responded to personal approaches by the UGM. Clinical service managers and senior managers were appointed. Clinical service directors and managers together began to examine the kind of management

Figure 2.2 The organisational structure

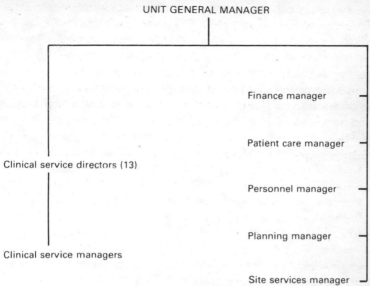

UNIT GENERAL MANAGER

Finance manager

Patient care manager

Clinical service directors (13)

Personnel manager

Planning manager

Clinical service managers

Site services manager

structures they needed to develop to reflect the unique nature of each service. The unit finance manager began formulating and discussing draft financial and manpower allocations for each clinical service. Discussion took place on the format of financial monitoring reports, and financial guidelines were established so that clinical service directors and managers understood the limits of their authority.

Establishing clear communication processes was important and through these the management structure was reinforced, to avoid the development of a direct relationship between unit general manager and clinical service managers which could effectively by-pass the clinical service directors.

2.2.9 *Training*

Resources were set aside for management development and training. The UGM held 'time out' sessions for clinical service directors and managers to help them to understand their roles, responsibilities and relationships. Study days, open to all, were held on topics such as understanding financial information, planning, quality promotion, managing sickness and absence, press and public relations. Some individuals attended external management courses geared to their personal development.

2.2.10   *The end of the beginning*

Two and a half years on, the unit has reached the end of the beginning of the new management structure. It is time to stop for a moment, take stock and determine the way forward for the next three to five years. Looking back over the problems and issues may provide some useful lessons for other managers who are reviewing or devising management arrangements.

2.3   Problems and solutions

2.3.1   *Where to begin*

The management structure is not an end in itself but a means to achieving the objectives of the service. The first task is to identify the objectives of the organisation. In the case study, the UGM did this by talking to staff and by looking at the district health authority's strategic and annual operational plans. Other approaches could have included reviewing, updating or, if none existed, producing a 'mission statement' and also consulting with consumers of services provided. It is important to talk through and test ideas with colleagues and senior managers at all stages of the development of the management structure. Outside testing is also helpful with peer groups or facilitators from academic centres or external organisations.

The UGM did not think through clearly or communicate the processes by which the proposals would be shared, final decisions made and the structure implemented. This would have helped minimise uncertainty in the organisation, particularly for staff whose posts were potentially under threat.

2.3.2   *Activities, decisions and relationships analyses*

The UGM considered the type of activities which were the focus of the organisation's business and examined different ways of grouping them. Thought was also given both to the decisions needed to achieve the organisation's objectives and how they should be made, and to relationships within the structure. Although recognising the problem of span of control, the UGM nevertheless decided to manage directly 13 clinical service directors and five senior managers. A structure with the minimum number of management levels was created, in order to shorten the line of communication between the UGM and the delivery of care. However, in practice, such an extensive span of control caused problems in adequately monitoring the performance of managers.

The issue of who should be appointed as managers of services was divisive and time consuming. Clearer definition of the role and responsibilities of the clinical service managers and mandatory provision of nursing professional advice within each service might have helped avoid this problem.

The structure provided no formal mechanism for bringing together clinical service directors and senior managers to benefit mutually from each other's advice and from which the UGM could derive the best possible management and clinical advice on any issue. This denied senior managers the opportunity to contribute corporately and to be aware of clinical opinion in the Unit. The clinical management board could have been expanded to include the five senior managers but this would have created a potentially unmanageable board of more than 20 members. Alternatively, a general management board could have been established with the UGM, the five senior managers and the chairman of the clinical management board, but this would have created duplication and possible conflict.

A balance needs to be achieved in grouping activities in a logical and focused way, yet maintaining a practicable number of second-in-line managers who are all afforded the opportunity to contribute in a corporate way.

2.3.3 Line and staff relationships

Considerable care was needed in the relationship between line and staff managers because of the potential for conflict, frustration and abrogation of responsibility. The line manager may become so dependent on the advice of a staff manager that he becomes unsure of his authority and seeks the staff manager's approval of his actions. Alternatively, the line manager may ignore the advice of the staff manager, who then becomes frustrated at his lack of effectiveness in getting his ideas or advice put into action. The UGM found that the key to satisfactory relationships was to ensure that each manager clearly understood his or her responsibilities, role and relationships, and to maintain good communications.

2.3.4   *Professional advice*

The major opposition to the management arrangements arose from professional attitudes within the health service. The NHS has a unique management culture as a result of the professional independence of clinicians and the employment of a large number of professionals. Managers come from a variety of backgrounds and their management responsibilities require them to make arrangements for the proper provision of professional advice in decision-making. In devising a management structure it is essential to determine at what level the management of the professions by the professions is needed, and at what level general management skills, rather than a body of specialist knowledge, are required.

However, all managers would do well to heed the warning of Robert Maxwell and the late Tom Evans who emphasised the need for all NHS general managers to understand, work with and gain trust from all health professionals.

2.3.5   *A framework*

From the case study and problems identified, a framework can be drawn which may be of help to managers facing the challenge of developing or reviewing a management structure. This is shown in Figure 2.3.

2.4   General principles

Successful management of any organisation depends on the development of a soundly based structure which underpins the organisation's business. It should provide a chart or map

Figure 2.3 Framework for developing or reviewing a management structure

1. IDENTIFY OBJECTIVES	What should be the business of the organisation?
2. ANALYSE THE ORGANISATION'S ACTIVITIES	How can the activities be grouped? Which activities belong together? How much emphasis should each activity have?
3. IDENTIFY THE DECISIONS NEEDED	What decisions are needed to achieve the organisation's objectives? What kind of decisions are they? At what organisational level should they be made? By whom? Who should participate in making the decisions?
4. IDENTIFY RELATIONSHIPS	What are the relationships between each part of the organisation? Which managers are 'consumers' of other managers' services?
5. DETERMINE WHICH ACTIVITIES ARE 'LINE' AND WHICH 'STAFF'	Which functions have direct responsibility for achieving the organisation's objectives? Which functions exist to provide advice and service?
6. DETERMINE REQUIREMENTS FOR PROFESSIONAL ADVICE	What professional advice is needed? At what level?

through which that business can be planned, directed and controlled. Clarity and simplicity are crucial.

The following general principles can be applied in devising or reviewing a management structure:

- Determine the objectives of the organisation, covering the main areas of activity
- Consider the environment within which the organisation will operate and ensure it is structured flexibly to accommodate change

- Highlight key activities which need resources and control and group them logically
- Determine which decisions are most vital to the organisation's success and who takes them
- Identify which separate organisational components should be established
- Identify the relationship of each part of the structure to the others
- Determine the number of levels required in the organisation and relate this to the optimum span of control
- For each job within the structure, clearly define the responsibility and authority attached to it
- Ensure clear lines of authority and accountability exist at and through all levels
- Determine what staff functions are required to support line managers
- Determine what professional advice is needed at each level of the organisation and how it will be provided
- Ensure provision is made to meet the information needs of each level of the organisation to facilitate managerial decisions
- Provide adequate communications throughout the organisation both during the process and as part of the proposals themselves

A good organisational structure will not, of itself, ensure the success of the organisation but it will provide a sound basis. Managers in the NHS, faced with the search for excellence in the delivery of preventive, diagnostic and therapeutic care within finite resources, must examine their organisations. They must be prepared to take risks, try new ideas and devise creative and thoughtful ways for improving health care. This can only be achieved by establishing a firm organisational foundation which the staff understand. It is this which will provide a milieu in which committed and enthusiastic staff can be supported in providing high quality services.

Bibliography

G. Best, *General Management: An audit for commitment and action* (Bristol: National Health Service Training Authority: Occasional Papers 1, 1984)

G.Best, 'Secrets of Success for Happy Families', *Health and Social Service Journal* (26 September 1985).

P. F. Drucker, *The Practice of Management*, revised edn (London: Heinemann and Pan, 1972)

T. Evans and R. Maxwell, *Griffiths: Challenge and Response* (King Edward's Hospital Fund for London, 1984)

R. Stewart, *The Reality of Organization* (London: Heinemann and Pan, 1972)

R. Stewart, *The Reality of Management*, revised edn (London: Heinemann and Pan, 1979)

I. Wickings (ed.) *Effective Unit Management* (King Edward's Hospital Fund for London, 1983)

A. Young, *The Manager's Handbook* (London: Sphere Books, 1986)

3
Managing People
Averil Dongworth

3.1 Introduction

'Managing people' can be described as the directing and controlling of staff to ensure the achievement of the organisation's goals. Any organisation, whether private company or public service, must recognise people as its most valuable asset if it is to be successful. The National Health Service is no exception; over three quarters of its total expenditure is made up of salaries and, as the largest single employer in Europe, it is vital that its managers have the skills to manage people effectively.

Many managers from a professional background who have managed staff have found the transition from functional management to general management to be difficult. However the fundamental principles are common to both and are illustrated in the case study.

3.2 Case study

In April 1986 Ann was promoted from nursing officer to the post of patient services manager in a large district general hospital. This was a new post bringing together, for the first time, different groups of staff under one manager. Ann had often been frustrated in the past at her inability to get things done because of the number of managers who had to be consulted. She felt that at last she would be able to 'get things moving'.

The unit general manager (UGM) to whom she was accountable was keen to reduce the length of waiting time in the outpatients department. This had been highlighted in the unit's annual review as a persistent problem which had given rise to many complaints. The UGM also made it very clear that the solution must be achieved within the allocated budget.

Three months after taking up post, Ann received a complaint via the UGM from a patient who had experienced a two-hour wait in the outpatients department before seeing a doctor. Furthermore he then discovered that he was attending the wrong clinic. He had been forced to return home and to make another appointment.

Ann felt that this was the perfect opportunity to make some changes. She arranged to meet the outpatient manager (OPM) and delivered an ultimatum: two-hour waiting times were 'not good enough' and would no longer be tolerated. In future no patient should wait longer than half an hour after his appointment time.

The OPM, whose background was in medical records, tried to explain that there were problems with the new computer system and that several patients had inadvertently been booked to see the wrong doctor. She said that the appointments staff were taking a long time to become competent with the computer with the result that they had to keep the manual system running in tandem. Moreover the medical staff insisted on seeing a set number of patients at each session, regardless of diagnosis, and so it was impossible to run an efficient appointment system. Ann replied that the OPM must ensure that appointments were made correctly and that she was to tell the medical staff that the correct numbers were to be booked in future. Despite the lack of any real discussion, Ann believed she had clarified her views and reported to the UGM that she expected to see a big improvement.

About two weeks later the UGM asked to see Ann. The consultant medical staff had told him that they anticipated an increase in waiting lists, as 'management' had instructed consultants to reduce the number of patients they saw in their outpatient clinics. He had said that he had given no such instruction and asked Ann for an explanation. Ann said that she had requested that correct numbers be booked in order to avoid long waiting times for patients. He then informed her that she must reduce waiting times without increasing the length of the waiting list.

Ann felt thoroughly demotivated; nothing had been mentioned about waiting lists until then. She went to see the outpatient manager again who said she was going to resign. She had tried to do all that had been asked of her, but felt that the situation was impossible.

The appointments staff were finding it impossible to find the time to develop their computer skills, and keeping the manual system operational was causing much confusion. Several of the staff had left and she was finding it difficult to recruit new people, although she had been able to persuade some of the filing clerks to fill in.

Nor could she any longer face the constant arguing with doctors about the numbers of patients for their clinics. The medical staff stated that Ann had no authority to organise clinic sizes. The OPM did not feel that anything she had done in the past couple of weeks had contributed to improving the service to patients.

Ann asked the OPM not to resign but to work with her to find a solution.

3.3   Problems and solutions

The case study highlights important issues in managing people which are relevant at every level.

● Motivation
● Implementing change
● Problem solving
● Setting goals
● Action plans
● Individual performance review
● Staff development

3.3.1   Motivation

The influence of management on the motivation of staff cannot be underestimated. Staff choose particular jobs or professions for a variety of personal reasons, but their retention as a cohesive and effective workforce requires the continual rein-forcement of motivating influences by managers at all levels.

Motivators outside the sphere of professional job satisfaction and peer support include recognition by managers of the staff contribution to the overall 'business' of the organisation.

Such recognition starts with the simple acknowledgement of a task well done. But more importantly the manager's role is to recognise the expertise of his staff in various spheres, and to involve them at an early stage in making decisions in areas where they have experience or where they may expect to be affected by the decision.

It is equally the manager's role to recognise those areas where staff are weak in experience or ability and to work positively with them to develop the skills they lack.

Involvement in decision making and development opportunities are both strongly motivating influences which reinforce the sense of purpose and pride in achievement which leads to successful working practice.

When Ann left the general manager's office she felt demotivated. The effort she had made to improve waiting times had been for nothing. When she met with the OPM, Ann found that she too was feeling demotivated, as were the appointments staff, some of whom had already resigned.

What could each of the characters in the case study have done to motivate their staff?

The UGM could have built up a motivated team by sharing with them his vision for the future of the unit, and ensuring that they all knew his goals. He could have made clear his stance on mistakes – that he would make allowances for mistakes, provided that lessons were learned – and he could have demonstrated that he was available for help and advice. He might also have declared his share of the blame for not communicating effectively with Ann.

If the UGM had adopted a more open style of management, it is likely that Ann would have behaved similarly, thus ensuring that her staff felt committed to the success of the unit. Consciously or subconsciously, staff do look to their managers as role models, particularly when, like Ann, they are new in post and not yet confident in their own abilities. Personal style is often copied from one's senior managers. Consequently, one of Ann's early meetings with the OPM was to demand improvements, reflecting her own experience with the UGM to some extent. The OPM must have been greatly discouraged to be criticised from the outset by her manager, who failed to take account of current problems.

It is probable that the OPM transferred her feelings to the appointments staff when she discussed their problems. It is hardly surprising that mistakes continued and staff resigned. She could have asked them for suggestions on how to find time for training. Staff like to be consulted and often have greater insight into solving problems than managers who are not so actively involved. Had they been involved in the problem solving process, they would have felt not that they were being criticised but that they had a useful contribution to make in improving the system.

Demotivating factors in any work setting are lack of involvement and lack of personal development. Managers should ensure that initiative is recognised and rewarded. First impressions of the case study might suggest a lack of initiative, yet Ann did grasp the opportunity to make changes which she believed to be valid. Since the results were so unsatisfactory, it is not surprising that her manager failed to reward the initiative. But if Ann is to have the confidence to take further decisions, her initiative should at least be recognised. As her manager, the UGM should use this opportunity to discuss and formulate with Ann a programme of personal development in relation to his plans for development of the unit as a whole.

Nor do achievements have to be measured in terms of major impact. The manager who has kept a busy outpatients department operational when there are problems such as staff shortage and changes in working practices has achieved much. The good manager will not allow any achievement to go unrewarded – a word of thanks and appreciation may be all that is required to motivate staff to continue their efforts.

3.3.2   Implementing change

Chapter 12 deals with this topic in depth, but from the case study it is clear that if a manager wishes to make changes, it is not enough to find fault with the current system and then issue instructions to do things differently. Ann would have been better advised to discuss possible changes with the staff involved, and, having considered all the advantages and disadvantages, sought their support before implementing them.

Instead, she started with a fixed view of what she wanted to change and, when the patient's complaint arrived, seized on it as justification for making the changes she saw as desirable. Although she had identified the outcome of the changes she wished to make, she had not considered the processes involved.

3.3.3 Problem solving

Managers spend a high percentage of their time solving problems and staff who are accountable to a manager quite reasonably expect that they will be able to obtain help and advice when problems occur. In the case study, the outpatient manager tried to tell Ann about several difficulties she was experiencing; first with the new computer system and second with doctors insisting on seeing a set number of patients in each session. From Ann's response it is difficult to know if she heard or understood the problems. With no discussion of these concerns she repeated her instructions.

What could Ann have done differently?

- Could she have listened more carefully to the outpatient manager?
- Would it have been possible to find out more about the problems?
- Was it within the scope of the outpatient manager's authority to deal with them?
- Should Ann have opened the discussion with the doctors?

It is not necessarily desirable for Ann to solve the problems for her outpatient manager but, as a senior manager, she has a responsibility to understand those problems and to offer constructive advice. Careful questioning could have elicited both the real problems with the new computer system and the motives of the doctors in insisting on a set quota of patients. In this way, Ann would have been more aware of the implications of what she was asking of her manager. They could have discussed the action required, who should take it, and when. They could have reached agreement on the action, and Ann would have been able to ensure the outpatient manager's ownership of the problems.

3.3.4 Setting goals

If, at the end of their first meeting goals had been agreed, the subsequent events could have been very different. The agreement of future goals to be reached within an agreed time period is essential to the manager–subordinate relationship. When establishing objectives for a subordinate the manager should ensure that they are:

● Specific
● Realistic
● Acceptable
● Measurable
● Known
● Understood
● Time bounded

The manager has a responsibility to ensure that objectives meet these criteria. It is not enough to say that all outpatients should be seen within half an hour of their appointment time, without first finding both the percentage of patients to be waiting for more than half an hour, an hour, one and a half hours, etc, and the reasons for the delays. Once this type of information is available it is possible to set objectives:

● To reduce the waiting time in outpatient clinics by 15 minutes for all patients waiting more than half an hour past their waiting time
● To produce a plan to reduce all waiting times to less than half an hour of appointment time, within one year

This approach is more realistic and the subordinate is more likely to agree to it as she knows exactly what is expected of her. Objectives must be precise and the use of vague terms such as 'increase', 'decrease' and 'optimise' should be avoided. It is important that the manager thinks through exactly what he wants achieved, communicates it effectively and ensures it is agreed.

3.3.5 Action plans

Once objectives have been agreed, the subordinate requires

time to reflect and think through the process she might use to achieve success. An action plan should be drawn up and discussed with the manager, providing an opportunity for the manager to analyse the logic of the plan. If this had occurred, Ann might well have realised that the outpatient manager's plan would have consequential effects (for example, increasing the waiting list) and this would have given rise to further thought about the problem.

However, it was only when the UGM brought it to her attention that Ann was aware of the effect of her instructions. She was new to the job and believed that the UGM wanted waiting times reduced. But he had not agreed that goal with her. Had he done so, he would have ensured that she knew that reducing the waiting list was also a priority and they would have discussed the best way of ensuring the doctors' commitment to making the necessary changes. If the goal had been agreed, Ann would have had more confidence in implementing change, since she would have had the opportunity to discuss the issues relating to the changes. More importantly, she would have been able to choose her timing rather than wait for an opportunity such as a complaint before raising the subject with her staff. In this situation Ann could have used the complaint to gather vital information about waiting times, the appointment system, and the doctors' role in deciding clinic size. Having that type of information would have enabled her to discuss with her UGM the correct action and a realistic target.

The concept of management by objectives [goals] is not new, but has only recently been given a high profile in the health service. It is important that if staff are to perform their jobs effectively, they should know what they are trying to achieve and why. All members of the unit management team should be aware of each other's objectives. The UGM needs to ensure that everyone in the team has complementary objectives or goals, so they can all work with the same purpose.

3.3.6 *Individual performance review (IPR)*

If the setting of objectives is to be effective then it is important that evaluation takes place. Individual performance review [related to pay] was introduced to the National Health Service in

1986 for general managers and, more recently, for other senior managers. The principles involved, however, can be applied at all levels of the organisation. The aims of individual performance review are:

● To improve job performance through changes in behaviour
● To let the subordinate know how she is performing, thus eliminating tension and anxiety
● To discuss means of improvement and development of potential by setting specific and realistic objectives and the means of measuring their achievement

The individual and the manager have an equal role to play, working together in a purposeful way that could justifiably be described as joint performance review. Individual performance review can be viewed as a cycle of events taking place over an agreed period of time – usually 6–12 months. The cycle consists of:

● Setting goals
● Action planning
● Major performance review
● Periodic reviews

Since goal setting and action planning have already been discussed, consideration will now be given to the review process. The major performance review interview is held at the end of one cycle and the start of the next and periodic reviews are held at regular intervals during the cycle to monitor progress.

The major performance review interview provides the manager and the subordinate with the opportunity to review progress to date. The review interview is a crucial element in successful management development. It is from information obtained at the interview that much of the subsequent planning for training and career development stems. It is therefore crucial that the interview is properly conducted.

If objectives have been achieved, then the interview can be fairly straightforward; if they have not, then the manager has to be skilful in determining the causes. She must not jump to conclusions and allocate blame, and it is vital that open and frank discussion takes place.

The causes of failure to achieve an objective might include:

- An objective which was too complex for the level of skills so far acquired by the subordinate
- Relevant surrounding circumstances had changed
- Inadequate effort by the subordinate to achieve the required results

Whatever the reason, it is important that a common understanding is reached. It is an occasion when the subordinate can discuss with the manager any difficulties encountered, and can bring to her attention ways in which the manager could have helped. A performance review interview needs to be conducted with great skill or it can easily turn into a cosy chat, a disciplinary meeting, or a counselling interview. The need for preparation and planning cannot be overstressed. There are two parties to a review meeting and both need to be given time to prepare.

Before the meeting the manager should restudy the job and review the personnel record of the subordinate, taking into consideration her work environment and any effects it may have on what appear to be personal failings, for example organisational difficulties. The manager should be clear about what she wishes to achieve. She should go to the interview with a flexible plan and an outline approach. The subordinate should prepare with self-evaluation of her performance during the period under review.

The meeting should be arranged at a time convenient to both parties, and adequate time should be allowed so that there is no pressure to rush through issues that require full discussion. During the meeting the subordinate should be encouraged to talk and describe her feelings and attitudes towards the job. She should be given the opportunity to analyse her own performance, evaluate achievements and make suggestions for improvements. The manager should be prepared to hear criticism of her own performance if the subordinate feels that this has inhibited her ability to perform at the desired level (for example, lack of guidance from the manager). The key to a successful review interview is the manager's ability to listen. The most common failure of managers conducting review interviews is that they do all the talking. At the end of the meeting (or at a follow-up meeting if preferred), new targets and action plans for achieving them should be agreed. After the meeting, the subordinate should feel she has been fairly treated, and both parties should have a clear understanding of how they have performed so far.

Unfortunately in the case study, neither the UGM nor Ann had thought enough about what they were doing to enable them to set objectives or allow time for review.

It is also important that periodic reviews are held, so that progress can be monitored and help and advice given where necessary. This will provide the subordinate with the opportunity to discuss any unforeseen problems that have arisen, possibly due to organisational changes, that could render the objective unattainable. The manager must always be flexible and prepared to negotiate and, if necessary, change the objective. Without periodic reviews there is a danger that subordinates struggle to achieve something that is either not within their authority or that they have not the confidence or ability to complete. The periodic review allows the subordinate to 'open up' to the manager without fear of being assessed and can act as a useful model for relationship building.

Managers therefore have to consider the following issues in relation to individual performance review:

● Do all your managers have goals/objectives for the next 6–12 months?
● Are these goals clearly stated so that you and your managers can have no misunderstanding as to their meaning?
● Do your managers know your goals?
● Do your managers know each others' goals?
● Have you set regular dates for your managers' performance review interviews?

3.3.7   Staff development

One of the prime responsibilities a manager has towards his staff is to develop them to their full potential. Yet so often managers forget, or are insufficiently aware of, the need for staff development. Investment in staff development will enable staff to do their job to the highest standard, benefiting the organisation in terms of efficient and effective performance. It also benefits the individual by giving her the tools to do the job – knowledge and skills. In recent years, managers' development has been singled out for special attention, but this should not be at the expense of other staff groups.

In the case study, the appointments staff clearly needed developing. They were having to cope with learning a totally new skill (computer operating) while still maintaining the old system to ensure that the service was maintained.

It is hardly surprising, therefore, that mistakes were made. The OPM had recognised the need for training while Ann seemed oblivious to it. A period of staff training in computer skills away from work would have caused difficulties for the OPM in the short term, and might have cost some money on Ann's budget, but the staff would more rapidly have become competent at operating the computer. It would also have shown them that management understood their problems and that they were valued. Fewer patients would have been given wrong appointments, and less time and money consumed in wasted effort.

It could be argued that staff development was being provided in the case study, but only in the most unplanned manner, causing considerable stress to Ann and the OPM. They were certainly learning the hard way. Every decision they made produced unwanted results: staff resigning; the doctors insisting that waiting lists would be increased; the displeasure of the UGM. But the learning experience should not be as uncomfortable as this. Of course everyone learns from their mistakes, but if every decision turns out to be a mistake, then the willingness of that person to make decisions will be greatly reduced. The UGM may have thought he was developing Ann by allowing her to get on with the job. He had promoted her from nursing officer to patient services manager and perhaps felt that the best way to develop her in that role was to see if she would 'sink or swim'.

Most staff development takes place on the job; that is to say, processes transpire which shape the development of an individual though they were not deliberately planned for this purpose. Had the UGM considered the substantial changes in Ann's role, he might have realized that she had definite development needs. She had been a professional managing a group of her professional colleagues for many years, and she understood what made them 'tick'.

Now she had general management responsibilities for various groups of staff and, although she had had contact with these groups during her professional career, she did not really know or understand them. The post was a new one and the UGM should have clarified his expectations of the role, identified the interdependence of members of the work group (nurses, doctors, appointments staff), and resolved any conflict associated with role ambiguity.

He should have ensured that he clarified Ann's needs by:

● Identifying her actual level of performance
● Identifying the desired level of performance
● Identifying immediate and long term training needs by comparing the difference between the actual and the desired levels

Causes of discrepancies between actual and desired performance can be organisational, environmental, motivational, or deficiencies in knowledge or skills. The manager has a responsibility to determine how his subordinates would benefit from development activities. If the issues can be discussed as early as possible, the scene is set for future openness, and the seeds have been sown for the development of mutual trust and respect. It is unwise for a manager to assume that a successful appointee has all the necessary skills to function effectively in a new post. The brightest of people need time to grow into a job. It is the senior manager's job to 'coach' the new manager by providing practical help and support. This does not imply that the manager should do the job of his subordinate, but it does mean that allowances have to be made for mistakes, which may have to be shouldered by the manager.

3.4 Summary

Since the introduction of general management to the NHS, much has been expected of its managers. Extra responsibilities, with increasing pressure to deliver results within very short time scales, have transformed the roles of many managers. They are expected to make more decisions at grassroot levels, and are held accountable for their actions. It has created an environment where managers can achieve, develop and grow.

The case study has highlighted that managers new to this environment need to be supported by their senior managers, and that they must be allowed to make their mistakes in a controlled environment. Senior managers have a responsibility to develop new managers, and ensure that learning experiences are as enjoyable as possible.

The individual performance review process, if properly handled, can give feedback and a sense of achievement and direction to all staff. It is a time consuming exercise and many managers may think it not worthwhile, but people are our most valuable asset, and to gain the full benefit of that asset, is worth considerable investment of time.

Bibliography

Aat Brakel, *People and Organisations Interacting*. (New York: Wiley, 1985).
Robert M. Frame *et al.*, *The Organizational Development Source Book, A Practitioner's Guide* (San Diego, Univ. Associates, 1982).
Charles Handy, *Understanding Organisations* (Harmondsworth: Penguin, 1985).
J. M. Kouzes, and B. Z. Posner, *The Leadership Challenge* (London: Jossey Bass, 1987).
M. London, *Developing Managers: A Guide to Motivating and Preparing Managers for Successful Managerial Careers* (London: Jossey Bass, 1985).
H. Mintzberg, *The Nature of Managerial Work* (New Jersey: Prentice Hall, 1980).
C. Molander, *Management Development: Key Concepts for Managers and Trainers* (Bromley, Chartwell-Bratt, 1986).
Rosemary Stewart, *The Reality of Management* (London: Pan Books, 1986).
Valerie and Andrew Stewart, *Managing the Poor Performer* (London: Gower, 1981).
George F. Thomason, *A Textbook of Personnel Management* (London: Institute of Personnel Management, 1981).
Derek Torrington, *Face to Face in Management* (New Jersey: Prentice Hall, 1982).
Mike Woodcock and Dave Frances, *The Unblocked Manager* (London: Gower, 1982).

4
Making Use of Information
Jolyon Vickers

4.1 Introduction

'It is of great importance in order to gain assured knowledge of things, to rely on exact acquaintance with facts, rather than on the uncertain testimony of public rumour; and then what we have proved for certain, we may proclaim without hesitation.' (St Bernard Letter, 12th century).

A vast amount of information is currently being collected and used within the National Health Service. The problem is often not so much a lack of information, but knowing how to use what is available, to understand the implications behind the figures, and to be able to present the findings in a manner which can be understood by the target audience.

The National Health Service is going through a major revolution in information collection. For the first time since its inception in 1948, there is a data dictionary which is being constantly updated and provides definitions for each of the data items. This in turn will encourage the collection of comparable data within district health authorities and in turn lead to more credible performance indicators (health service indicators).

It is important, however, to be able to understand the significant differences between pre- and post-Körner figures if suspect trends are to be avoided.

Following increasing unhappiness with the nature of data collection in the National Health Service, which, because of the changed trends in health care delivery, did not capture the true nature of hospital and community workloads, Edith Körner was asked to chair a steering group to consider health service information.

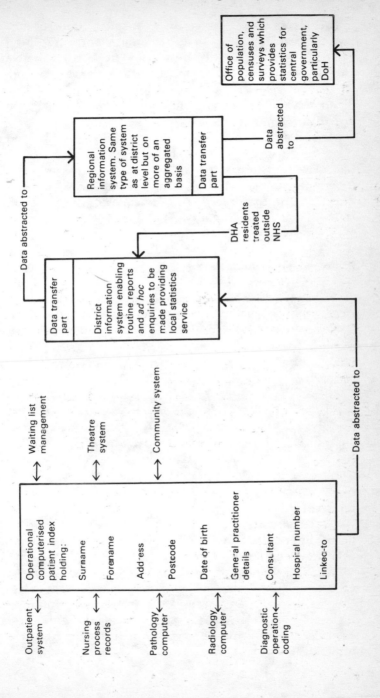

Figure 4.1 An example of an operational system feeding a data collection/information production process

The steering groups covered hospital, community, manpower, transport, and financial information. The group met between 1980 and 1984, producing six reports for the National Health Service. It recommended that, wherever possible, data should be collected as a by-product of normal work activity, illustrated (Figure 4.1) by the work of the interactive patient administration system.

Many district health authorities have not been able to implement this recommendation because of shortages of suitable hardware, software, staff skills, staffing resources etc. Interim or long term manual data collection systems have therefore been introduced in their place. The principles of the minimum data set are explained in Figure 4.2.

Figure 4.2   The principles of a minimum data set, A data mountain

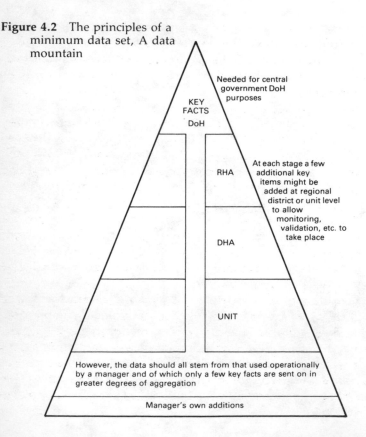

It is important to take time to establish the facts about a particular problem as St Bernard had so clearly recognised so many centuries ago. What has to be avoided is a headlong rush into resolving the problem, without the full facts being available.

Using the right information for the right purpose is a skill which needs to be developed and this can only be achieved from a thorough understanding of the data, how and where it is collected, why it is collected and by whom it is used at all levels in the NHS from the point of patient care delivery to the Houses of Parliament.

Data is the raw building block, which is then turned into information by the skills of collation, validation, manipulation, presentation, and interpretation.

- *Collation* involves scrupulous data collection methods by staff who are interested and understand their valuable role – this might include manual addition from recorded observations or the use of calculators, optical mark reader cards or computers
- *Validation* is the skill of ensuring that the data is of good quality and correctly calculated both for internal consistency (that all the columns add up correctly and are completed where relevant) and also that unexplained trends and variances from previous observations are not introduced and that conflicting items are not present (for instance, day cases staying for ten days in hospital)
- *Manipulation* is the skill of taking the raw data from one or more data sets to produce a spread sheet to calculate trends and 'what if' scenarios. Spread sheets are computer based worksheets that have largely replaced the need to summarise and calculate data on paper
- *Presentation* is all important – data can be sound and well calculated, but if it is presented on a mass of complicated, smeared graphs and 'busy' tables, few managers will take time to read them and will simply ask for more information.
- *Interpretation* is allied to presentation and shows the manager a sound understanding of the data, with the ability to foresee trends and patterns and without trying to obscure any of the facts

From time to time, you may be asked by your staff to explain why data (routine or *ad hoc*) is being collected – 'Who uses these figures?' As a senior manager you need to develop your understanding of how data and information are used for such things as resource allocation, quality assurance, epidemiological studies, health promotion and disease prevention programmes and for measuring the efficiency and effectiveness of health care.

You may also find that some data items are not routinely collected. You should therefore try to develop skills in *ad hoc* data collection, including sampling and surveys.

4.2   Case study

Plaxtol General Hospital is a 300 bed district general hospital serving a semi-rural district with a population of 195000. The population is of average age, sex and structure compared with national norms for England and Wales. The district general hospital, built in 1984 on a green field site, is on the outskirts of the market town. The district has one centre of population, Plaxtol, the remaining area being extensively rural, with a number of small or medium sized villages and farms.

You have recently been appointed as ambulatory care manager from outside the district health authority. Your responsibilities will cover the accident and emergency services, outpatients, day case unit and the trauma wards with both nursing and clerical staff.

Your appointment has come at a difficult time when there have been complaints in the local press and media from general practitioners, the community health council and others about:

1. Long waiting times for outpatient appointments.
2. Delays in the A & E department for attention.

The anaesthetists are also concerned that inappropriate cases are being brought in for day case surgery, which should in their opinion have been brought into hospital as ordinary admissions.

You are keen to resolve these issues and get to the bottom of these problems, but are aware you will need the right information to assess priorities.

In addition, you would like to improve staff morale and commitment by providing variety in staff work patterns. This, you feel, will include introducing flexibility in staff allocation for both nurses and clerical staff. In turn you feel this should assist in providing holiday, sickness and study leave cover. You hope this will also enhance the skill levels of your staff.

4.3 Issues to be addressed

4.3.1 Demographic information

- Population statistics
  Small area statistics
  1981 census
  Projections
- Cross boundary flows for health authorities inpatients, any surveys that exist for accident and emergency department use, or data available from an operational computer system
- Patient flows, for instance, transport routes; natural migration patterns; holiday, university, boarding schools, seasonal flows

4.3.2 Staffing and service arrangements.

- Planning documents that exist about the building of your unit
- Service staffing levels
- Was it a level transfer or did this new district general hospital replace one or more old hospitals, were the staffing levels increased to take account of the new development, or was it assumed that the activity levels of the new hospital would be the same?
- What are the skill levels of your current staff, their strengths, their weaknesses, their development needs?

4.3.3. Staffing information

- The age distribution of your staff

- The skill mix
- The working hours' flexibility
- The current contractual position – are they contracted to work on one ward or more?
- Holiday rostering arrangements
- Learner allocation
- Potential postbasic course material

4.3.4   Outpatient clinic workload

- Is a long waiting time for an outpatient appointment a reflection of the clinical practice of discharging few patients back to the care of their general practitioner?
- Are the junior and medical staff on the six monthly rotation unwilling to discharge patients from outpatient clinics, preferring to give the patient a further review appointment when they will have moved on?
- Are a large proportion of your clinics consultant-initiated attendances?
- Are there mistaken assumptions of high 'did not arrive' rates at your clinics with the result that clinics are overbooked and now almost always overrun?

4.3.5   A & E workload

- Are delays in the accident and emergency department caused by a mismatch between staffing and predicted workload?
- Are too many of your patients coming back to the accident and emergency department who could be better seen in outpatient clinics, for example burns/dressings/fractures. Could these be scheduled and staffed accordingly?
- Is the work in your department seasonal?
- Does it fluctuate during the week?
- Does it fluctuate during the day?
- What is the proportion of new attendances versus re-attendances?

4.3.6   Day case workload

- What sort of patients are coming for day case surgery?

- Have you examined how many day case patients are transferred to the main wards, remaining overnight because of
  their clinical condition?
- How long have your day cases been waiting before admission? Perhaps their condition warranted day case interven-
  tion at the time of appointment, but a year later on, when
  they are admitted, they might well have been more appropriately treated as an ordinary admission
- What preoperative anaesthetic assessment arrangements are
  being made?
- Are patients being transferred from the ordinary admission
  waiting list to the day case waiting list because of long
  standing financial or bed availability problems which, though
  intended in good faith to assist the patient, are in fact exacer-
  bating the problem?

Figure 4.3   Look at a problem all the way round ⎯⎯⎯⎯→

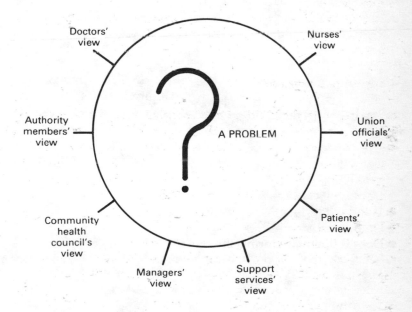

⎯⎯⎯⎯→ it may look different from the other side

Catalogue the existing problems:

● Are they inter-related?
● What are the differing views (see Figure 4.3)
● Are they new problems?
● Are they long standing problems?

4.4   What information is available?

4.4.1   Körner minimum data set for consultant outpatient clinic activity.

Since 1 April 1987, each district health authority has been collecting a revised information set about outpatient clinic activity. Some district health authorities have installed computerised outpatient department management systems, either linked with their patient administration system or as stand-alone systems. These systems provide detailed profiles of the nature of the clientele of the outpatient service and enable age/sex analyses to be made as well as giving details about waiting times between referral, first appointment, and subsequent appointment.

At a minimum, each district health authority is required to collect the data items for the statistical return KH09. This details, by each specialty, the following information:

● The number of scheduled clinic sessions by specialty
● The number of clinic sessions by specialty that were scheduled but cancelled
● The number of referrals (new patients) who attended
● The number of referrals (new patients) who failed to attend appointments
● The number of re-attendances, who were asked to return by the consultant (now called consultant-initiated attendances)
● The number of re-attendances (consultant-initiated) who failed to attend for their appointment
● The number of referrals (new patients), who attended as a consequence of a GP or general dental practitioner referral letter

● The number of private patients attending during an NHS clinic
● The number of patients attending as a result of contractual arrangements

This minimum data set may well be supplemented at a regional, district or local level to capture such items as:

● Discharges from clinic (patients who are not given a further follow up appointment but are referred back to the GP)
● Procedures. (The number of technical procedures which are conducted. These indicate the additional work involved in outpatient department attendance over and above chaperoning duties)
● The waiting time for an outpatient appointment between referral and attendance. (The number of weeks a non-urgent patient waits for an appointment)
● The times of start and finish of clinic
● The number of staff in attendance

The above information should allow the manager to know what is going on.

4.4.2 Körner minimum data set for accident and emergency departments.

Again, like outpatients, an accident and emergency computer system may be installed, which should be able to provide detailed analyses of the clientèle using the department. However, at a minimum, the following will be collected for KH09 returns:

● New patients
● Follow-up attendances

These should, wherever possible, be collected on a daily or even a shift basis to be able to plot trends in activity, which in turn can be used to match staffing to workload.

4.4.3 Körner minimum data set for elective admissions

Again this may be a manual or computerised system, which at the minimum will be collecting:

- The number of people waiting, by specialty, for ordinary or day case admissions
- The number of people waiting with a set date and those without a date for admission
- The number of months that individuals have been waiting in months
- The number of people added to the list each quarter
- The number of people offered admission in the quarter and admitted
- The number of people offered admission in the quarter who either failed to arrive or whose admission was cancelled by the hospital
- The number of people who decline an offer of admission
- The number of people who are removed from this list other than for admission

4.4.4   Körner minimum data set for manpower

Again this may be partly or fully computerised, but the personnel department will advise on:

- The budgeted establishment of the department
- The skill profile for the various posts in the department
- The actual number/cost/skills of your staff in post

Often these will not correlate and part of your skill as a manager will be to develop the potential of your staff, by either on the job or off the job training, and to balance the distribution of these skills throughout the department.

4.4.5   Hospital clinical activity analysis

Following the April 1987 Korner implementation, more information is now available on the inpatients, both day and ordinary admissions, who have passed through hospitals in the district. This should be able to provide you with information about:

- The age/sex of your patients
- The length of stay for various diagnoses, coded according to the international classification of diseases (ICCD9)

● The nature of any operative procedures carried out on these clients which will again be coded according to the Office of Population Census and Surveys classification of procedures, fourth revision

● The length of time people have waited between being on the elective admission list and actually being admitted to hospital

These should allow comparisons to be made between consultants and specialties, and may in turn reflect different pre- and post-operative patient management regimes.

4.4.6 Population/demography/cross boundary flows

It is important to understand the nature of the population you are trying to serve. Detailed population figures called Small Area Statistics should be available in the district health authority and these will catalogue census details and are broken down by each electoral ward in the district.

Population projections are available from the Office of Population Census and Surveys. These are mid-year projections by district which show projected trends in global population growth by standard age bands and sex mix. Cross boundary flow is currently calculated only on inpatient admissions by using post codes to determine the district of origin of the patient. Often *ad hoc* A & E and outpatient surveys are then carried out, helping to predict the total cross boundary flows for these services. Eventually, once outpatient and A & E computer systems are available, this flow will be identified automatically.

4.5 Relevance of technology for gathering and generating information

In most instances, information technology is essential for data collection and information production. However, information technology is only a tool for collecting the data and producing the information. You need to ensure that you are able to convert the data into information easily with adequate manual backup procedures, and comply with the Data Protection Act (1984).

You must also ensure that you can accommodate modifications without difficulty.

It may be wise to let someone else do the piloting unless you feel completely able to support a pilot project with staff, skills, finance, etc. Software must be purchased before hardware.

4.6   How much, or how little, or how often?

You will need sufficient information to assist you in sorting out your problem, but you should discuss with your sources which items of collected data will clarify and not cloud the issue. You do not want to be swamped with masses of computer printout, neither do you want to miss a key fact.

Your information needs will vary according to the data set involved; for instance it may be useful to examine your A & E attenders by staff shift (night, early and late) to see if you have the staff balance correct, both during a 24-hour period and each day of the week. However, it would be excessive to have your outpatient figures on a daily basis. Monthly trends will be more than adequate, unless you have a detailed analysis to make.

4.7   Using the information

● Pictures tell a thousand words – graphs, pie, bar charts
● Highlight the key facts
● Avoid jargon
● Don't be afraid to make it appear simple. The general public, community health councils and authority members are not always familiar with procedures and terms and may simply ask for more information if they feel that the issue is being masked by technical language

Bibliography

General national data
GB Central Statistical Office, *Key Data* (London: HMSO, annual publication).
GB Central Statistical Office, *Social Trends*, (London: HMSO, annual publication).

Health services data
Birth Statistics, Mortality Statistics (London: OPCS)
Health and Personal Social Services Statistics (London: DHSS, annual publication).
John M. Yates, *Hospital Beds* (London: Heinemann Medical, 1982).
John Yates, *Why are we Waiting, An Analysis of Hospital Waiting Lists* (Oxford University Press, 1987).

Figures in general – presentation
Myra Chapman, *Plain Figures, Cabinet Office (Management and Personnel Office), Civil Service College,* (London: HMSO, 1986).

Statistics
W. M. Castle, *Statistics in Small Doses,* 2nd edn (London: Churchill Livingstone, 1976).
T. J. Hannigan, *Statistics* (London: Macmillan, 1987).
Aviva Petrie, *Lecture Notes on Medical Statistics,* 2nd edn (Oxford: Blackwell, 1987).
Derek Rowntree, *Statistics without Tears,* (*A primer for non-mathematicians*) (London: Penguin, 1981).

Körner
National Health Service in association with the Department of Health and Social Security, *User Guide to the 1st and 4th Reports of the Steering Group on Health Services Information* (London: HMSO 1984).
NHS/DHSS Steering Group on Health Services Information, Reports to the Secretary to State, *Reports 1 to 6 and the Supplement to the 1st and 4th Report* (London· HMSO, 1982 5).
Phil Windsor, 'Introducing Körner – a critical guide to the work and recommendations of the Steering Group on Health Services Information', *British Journal of Health Care Computing* (1986).

Surveys
C. A. Moser and G. Kalton, *Survey Methods in Social Investigations,* 2nd rev (London: Gower, 1985).
Abraham Naftali Oppenheim, *Questionaire Design and Attitude Measurement* (London: Heinemann Education/Gower Publications, 1968).

Performance indicators
Comparing Health Authorities 1983–86 (London: DHSS, 1986).

5

Setting and Managing a Budget
William Bryans

5.1 Introduction

With or without the advent of the general management culture, there has inevitably been a growing awareness of the need to control expenditure. This has been partly due to the increasing pressure on funding and partly due to initiatives taken by treasurers to provide mechanisms which enable the exercise of control.

This chapter shows how effective budgetary control techniques depend upon:

● Involvement in planning
● Understanding the budget system
● Choice and participation of budget holders
● Adequate target setting techniques
● Time frames and their use
● Controlling the overspending

Managers at all levels need to be aware of the condition of their total environment from both the resource point of view and the opportunities which exist in the field of general management for all professionals including nurses. A case study of the closure of a hospital illustrates various budgetary points but readers will observe other factors which influenced the situation.

The objective of the case study is to explore various aspects of budgetary control using a hospital closure to illustrate effects on:

● Patients
● Staff
● Estate
● Finance

5.2   Case study – the closure of Skegatilla hospital

5.2.1   *Background*

Skegatilla Hospital, one of two within the Skegatilla and Killybodagh Unit of Management (the other being Killybodagh
General Hospital) had a bed complement of 85 which was
allocated to the care of elderly people. During the financial year
ended 31 March 1986 there was an average bed occupancy of
99.55 per cent. Twenty-six patients were admitted during the
year and 42 were discharged or died. At the end of August 1986
the population had declined to 69 patients.

With the exception of two patients who came from Skegatilla,
the main origin of the patient population was the Killybodagh
area.

Permanent trained nursing staff were drawn from the Killybodagh area. The majority of ancillary and general staff lived
locally.

5.2.2   *The estate*

The hutted style accommodation was not suited to the care of
elderly people and the prefabricated structure, which was
designed as a temporary building for use during the war, had no
long-term future.

Pressing demands for expenditure were estimated to be in the
order of £120000. The hospital had not been rewired since its
opening and this work was therefore urgent. The sewage plant
was declining rapidly and was a potential health hazard.

5.2.3   *Staffing*

Over the years it had become increasingly difficult to recruit and
retain a permanent trained nursing and paramedical workforce.
This difficulty resulted in the lower patient population.

5.2.4   *Rationalisation*

Groups of caring staff moved with their patients to other vacant and/or redesignated accommodation. As far as nursing staff were concerned, no reductions were envisaged. However, most ancillary staff were not required.

5.2.5   *Financial implications/costings*

There was financial pressure on the unit to save £700000 and a study established the feasibility of rationalising hospital beds on one site at Killybodagh hospital. This study showed that in order to maintain or replace the existing Skegatilla Hospital, which was in poor condition, an investment of some £3.6 million was necessary but if the rationalisation option was adopted £373000 pa could be saved, contributing substantially to the funding deficit.

5.3   Involvement in planning

A financial or budget plan is an important facet of the overall planning exercise. Figure 5.1 is a simple illustration of plan making and demonstrates that, in matching strategic and operational demands, it seldom happens that adequate funds are available. The discrepancies often arise because of the funding methods:

● Cash limits – permitted level of inflation in the public sector
● Cash planning – effects of cash limits in future years
● Resource allocation – application of a formula which reallocates resources to 'less well off' regions and authorities

Budgets tend to fall short of inflation and a 2 per cent deficit in one year can become £340000 on a district budget of £17 million. Thus bids for new funds (which inevitably exceed available funds anyway) have to be considered together with a funding deficit. The dilemma must be resolved in some compromise which results in a different approach to the delivery of care.

Although there were other factors at Skegatilla, financial

Figure 5.1 Plan making

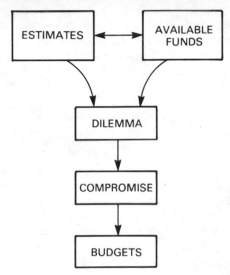

pressure to save £700000 made the rationalisation of hospital beds a priority and the closure of Skegalilla was suddenly justifiable.

Financial planning, involvement in the multidisciplinary planning cycle and the need for flexibility are crucial for budget managers so that good management practice pervades the organisation.

There must be involvement at all levels and throughout all disciplines in order to ensure that a comprehensive and realistic budget plan evolves. The following should be measured, and consensus achieved, in order to set financial objectives:

● Efficiency
● Economy
● Standards (or quality)

Reporting mechanisms cover deviations. Some deviations may be tolerable but, at an agreed level of deviation, a new plan may be necessary.

The balance between resource limitations and planned and

unplanned changes in demand creates a greater awareness of the effective use of services. Priorities for development (or, at worst, just to stand still) have to be weighed against existing service provision some of which might have to be abandoned or rationalised. Thus the fate of Skegatilla Hospital was sealed.

5.4   Understanding the budget system

5.4.1   *The budget plan*

It is clear that the budget plan is the product of the consultative (and sometimes prescriptive) mechanism through which we balance limited resources with perceived objectives. The plan embraces all resources including finance, but does not necessarily have to be expressed in financial terms: in other words it could be pairs of hands; rations; beds; sessions; and so on. The main characteristics are that:

● It is part of an agreed plan
● It has clear objectives to be achieved in a specific time span
● It provides a measure of achievement
● It responds to deviations

The Skegatilla and Killybodagh Unit faced a substantial funding deficit for the year 1986/87. After the feasibility study it was clear that, through the rationalisation of beds in Killybodagh, Skegatilla Long Stay Hospital should be closed. This was made possible through the opening of one 20-bed vacant ward and the redesignation of two surgical wards which had low occupancy rates. The length of stay suggested that they were non-acute: 72+9405 days in Killybodagh compared with the national average of 7·07 days (minimum 3·5, maximum 10·6 days).

It therefore became part of the unit's operational plan to close Skegatilla by October 1987 and the savings of £150000 in 1986/87 and £300000 in 1987/88 would be a contribution towards the deficit.

The condition of the estate was also a major consideration since spending was escalating on major maintenance works:

1979/80 — £19 000
1980/81 — £10 000
1981/82 — £17 000
1982/83 — £36 000
1983/84 — £25 000
1984/85 — £31 000
1985/86 — £15 000

And there was now a pressing demand for expenditure of £120 000 during 1986/87.

5.4.2   The budgetary control system

In order to implement any such plan a budgetary control system which is compatible with the plan is necessary. This means that the control mechanism must be expressed in the same mode as the plan; in other words with the same objectives, the same resource assumptions, the same time scales, etc.

A budgetary control system should:

● Exercise control
● Identify need to reallocate resources
● Demonstrate effective use of resources
● Exhibit flexibility to meet changing priorities

It usually consists of a series of statements to budget holders, and summaries to senior managers, which are intended to measure achievements and identify variations.

A simple statement will include:

Budget holder's name
Name of budget
Period of time
{ Target to date
Spending to date }

Continuous budget   Fixed budget
Variation shown   Remainder shown

A continuous budget is one which is subject to a more or less constant demand: its performance can therefore be measured by dividing it into equal portions to be compared with actual expenditure, say on a weekly, monthly or quarterly basis, thus producing a variable. Most payroll and material budgets are amenable. By observing an emerging pattern of progressive over or underspending, it is possible to assess an outcome and to amend activities so that an undesirable outcome is avoided.

Examples of fixed budgets are found in areas of demand which are known but are for the most part considered to be 'once and for all' or 'non-recurring'. The condition of the estate which over the years attracted major works would fall into this category. In this type of case, however, budget management cannot be monitored by segmenting money and time. It must be based on an assessment of what part of the project still has to be completed compared with how much time and money is left (the remainder).

5.5   Choice and participation of budget holders

Budgetary management can be viewed from two extreme points of view. On the one hand there is the status and control that it appears to bestow: on the other, an unwillingness to participate. The second situation seriously damages any system as the unwillingness can be due to a lack of comprehension, ability, application, confidence and commitment.

The first four can be overcome by training and supervision but the causes for lack of commitment are more difficult to detect and, therefore, much more difficult to rectify. Lack of commitment has been attributed to a number of factors:

● Effort not justified
● Other more worthwhile goals take priority
● Competition for scarce resources is distasteful
● Critical judgement impaired
● Information might be criticised for its quantity, quality or validity
● System is either limiting or demotivating

Managers must be aware of these political (small p) under-currents.

In general terms, the choice of budget holder can be made on the basis of:

● Facility – where the budget centre is (hospital)
● Profession – the mainstream profession (nursing)
● Discipline – specific type of work (midwifery)
● Function – what they do (delivery suite)

These choices may not always be compatible. For example if resources are divided by facility each profession within that facility will be competing for its slice of the facility cake. If on the other hand the basis is to be by profession, the chief professional may chose to move resources through facilities or across disciplines or functions (provided professional practice permits). This arrangement is called 'virement'. It is important therefore that a budget holder is clear about the ground rules as these will differ with circumstances and it is unusual to have a completely unified approach.

If the Skegatilla nursing officer's budget of £500000 was considered part of an overall nursing budget then all or part of that budget could be transferred elsewhere in the district nursing budget. On the other hand, if it were considered part of the unit budget then by agreement all or part of it could be used to support some other budget in the unit. Where there is confusion, there is also the danger that savings can be counted twice. Thus:

Savings to nursing budget	500000
Savings to unit budget	500000
	1000000

is clearly wrong yet it can and does happen.

In the case study there was a total facility budget for Skegatilla Hospital (see Table 5.1). An analysis of these budget holders (see Table 5.2) shows that although Skegatilla Hospital had a unit budget, with the exception of the nursing officer, who had a dedicated budget, the other composites were all part of a wider scene, in this case a group or sector budget.

Table 5.1   Budget for Skegatilla Hospital

	£000	£000	£000
Payroll			
Nursing officer	500		
Group catering manager	62		
Group domestic manager	54		
Group estate manager	18		
Sector administrator	16	650	
Goods and services			
Provisions (group catering mgr)	20		
Heat/light (group estate mgr)	40		
Rent and rates (sector administrator)	24		
Other (sector administrator)	38	122	772

Inherent in this is a dilemma with which managers are constantly confronted (consciously or unconsciously). On the one hand there is, or should be, the desire to delegate budget management as far down the line as possible. On the other, the smaller the budget, the more difficult it is to manage. The loss through sickness of three staff to both the nursing officer and the catering manager demonstrates this dilemma. Because of the number of staff in the nursing officer's budget (59) the loss of three nurses could probably be absorbed and result in a short-

Table 5.2   Budget holders at Skegatilla Hospital

Budget holder	Facility	Profession	Discipline	Function
Nursing officer	Skegatilla hospital	Nursing	Care of the elderly people	—
Group catering manager	,,	—	—	Catering
Group domestic services manager	,,	—	—	Domestic services
Group estate manager	,,	—	—	Estate
Sector administrator	,,	—	—	Admin. and support

term underspending. The catering manager, with a complement of only 10, would have to recruit more staff from elsewhere, or pay massive overtime, resulting in overspending. Thus there is always a delegation dilemma in attempting to obtain the maximum benefits to be derived from a compromise between delegation and budget size.

5.6   Adequate target setting techniques

Anyone could be forgiven for thinking that, once a base line has been established, and developments agreed, these, together with the ravages of inflation, should be funded in full. This ignores the budgetary control characteristics identified in 5.4.2 which are manifested in the:

● Exercise of control
● Identification of need to reallocate
● Demonstration of effective use of resources
● Exhibition of flexibility

It also ignores two basic facts which pertain in other facets of economic life. First, the householder who knows the likely income for a period is forced to plan family spending and activities in order both to live within the limits and to provide for contingencies. Second, in the business world, the risk element will dictate the level and structure of spending. These criteria can be applied to the NHS.

The main approaches to target setting are listed and briefly described below:

● Incremental crediting is the system whereby in the past a basic budget was uplifted to take full account of pay awards, price increases and any other agreed development money
● Programme planning applies where account is taken of the longer term as it applies to a particular care régime
● Cash limits and cash planning impose limits on budget setting. The distribution of resulting deficits can be an extremely delicate process
● Zero-based system embraces a whole system package which

allows the release of total funding only where the total can be justified. In other words each budget is reduced to zero and rebuilt at the beginning of each period. This is not widely used in the NHS

● Standards costed is where the standard or quality of the service to be provided has been clearly defined and agreed. It is possible thereafter to prepare a detailed costing which, if it can be afforded, would form the basis of a budget. Otherwise a redefinition of the standard would be necessary

Whatever approach is taken, it is clear that a relationship with workload is necessary. In the NHS, a major workload measure is the average cost of caring for one patient for one week. The classic case indicates that, with increasing occupancy, the average cost tends to fall because the overheads remain the same. However, when an optimum point is reached, more space, staff, goods, services, overheads have to be provided. This causes the average cost to rise again. Figure 5.2 illustrates this.

A budget could be constructed for any point on the curve. Taking point B, where the patient numbers P had an average cost of AC, the budget would be $P \times AC$.

In more practical terms Skegatilla Hospital, which was staffed for an optimum of 72 patients, would portray the graphical characteristics illustrated in Table 5.3.

Figure 5.2   Relationship of cost to workload

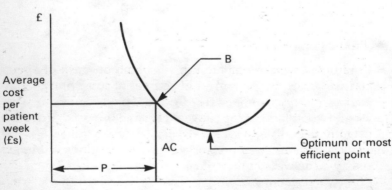

Table 5.3 Cost and workload at Skegatilla Hospital

Number of patients	18	36	54	72	90
Average cost per patient week (£)	412	276	230	206*	210†
Total possible patient weeks in one year	936	1872	2808	3744	4680
Budget (£000)	386	517	646	772	983

*Optimum
†Average cost begins to rise after optimum has been reached

Having set the target, few budgets conform to a regular pattern, and skill is needed to manage variations.

Where budgets can easily be divided over the total period, and accurate interim spending data is available, variation reporting may reasonably be relied on as a main indicator of spending trends, provided sight is not lost of the implications of decisions and commitments before the historical record. This is particularly relevant to day-to-day expenditure which tends to be a regular or continuous feature. Although it might be expected that these expenditure patterns would be constant, in fact they tend to fluctuate because of marginal activity. A number of factors, singly or in combination, can cause marginal activity. For example:

1. Delivery of materials or equipment.
2. Staff shortages.
3. Absenteeism.
4. Training programmes.
5. Production problems.

Confronted with the day to day or continuous task of operational management, the budget holder has to substitute alternatives in order to maintain the service. However this usually causes a deviation from the original plan and opportunities have constantly to be sought which will compensate, thus maintaining an expenditure pattern consistent with continuity of budget and service delivery.

When management of day-to-day or continuous budgets are observed frequent variations will be noticed.

5.7   Time frames and their use

It is important to budget for time as well as other resources. This is usually done through the definition of a variety of time frames within which it is intended to operate. These artificial time limits can then be used as a frequent measurement of both activity and achievement.

The time frame for the closure of Skegatilla Hospital was to be between June and September 1987 and the anticipated release of funds was £150000 in 1987/88 and £300000 in 1988/89.

It might be supposed that each time frame should receive an equal share of the overall budget or that the time frames should be artificially expanded or compressed to take account of un-equal increments. This latter concept is not as incredible as it sounds and is, for example, a familiar application in relation to hospital heating bills. In assessing budgetary viability, violent or dramatic changes in direction would suggest that the budget itself is too small. Similarly, lethargy in responding to control indicates either that activity at the margin cannot be regulated and a change in the rules is necessary, or that proper manage-ment of the budget is not taking place.

A gradual movement towards an increased overspending may, if unchallenged, result in a bid for an unauthorised im-proved budget base through a process of 'established practice'. On the other hand, a gradual drift towards an underspent position may prompt the notion that a lower budget base may be easily tolerated.

Although it would be impossible to make an absolute rule regarding these two characteristics, it might be reasonable to expect a small number of changes in direction in a budgetary period. The maximum variations would clearly be no more than the number of sub-divisions in the period. These changes would have a more or less balancing effect so that the cumulative variation tended to nil. In other words, the sum of the total overspendings in any time frame should tend to be cancelled out by the cumulative underspendings.

Consideration of the dramatic effect of fluctuations is even more difficult because every organisation will have its own idea of acceptable levels. In general terms it would seem impractical to go much further than to say that variations should be modest rather than dramatic.

5.8   Controlling the overspending

5.8.1   *The well managed budget*

A well managed budget implies a good understanding and control of the factors and contingencies already described. Within any time frame, however, while the core expenditure is under control, there is constant marginal activity about the target time. This is caused by a number of factors:

● Staff vacancies
● Overtime
● Weekend duty
● Sickness
● Temporary staff
● Over ordering
● Under or late deliveries
● Repairs
● Replacements
● Works
● Over or underestimates for contingencies
● Variations in workloads

The result is a tendency to overspend or underspend which has to be carefully monitored and managed through a process of reduction, or substitution.

As nursing represents 65 per cent of the total Skegatilla Hospital budget a closer look is worthwhile. (Table 5.4).

If one SEN and two nursing auxiliary vacancies occurred, an annual saving of around £23 000 would result – provided the posts were not filled. This could be used to:

1. Fund a deficit elsewhere.
2. Buy other staff.
3. Replace furniture and equipment.

Table 5.4   Nursing budget – Skegatilla Hospital

	FSL*	Basic cost	Weekend duty	Night duty	Bank holiday	Gross cost	Average cost
Senior nurses	1.0	15700	300	—		16000	16000
Sisters	4.6	57200	1400	1800	600	61000	13300
Staff nurses	11.0	94700	2000	2400	900	100000	9000
SENs	18.0	142400	2200	4200	1200	150000	8400
Auxiliaries	24.0	161300	6200	3000	2500	173000	7200
Totals	58.6	£471300	£12100	£11400	£5200	£500000	£8500

*Funded staff level (FSL) = the number and type of staff which *could* be bought with £500000

Its use for non-recurring purposes such as the purchase of furniture and equipment requires careful supervision because orders are seldom fulfilled within the time limit. As the time limit expires other orders are usually introduced and those unfulfilled are cancelled or carried forward into the new accounting period.

5.8.2   Variable workloads

These are unpredictable, but the matching of resources to workloads and patterns is an important key to good budget management. Such variations can result from:

● Change in the balance of care
● Greater emphasis on day surgery and day care
● Introduction of 5-day wards
● Holiday closures
● Planned and unplanned closures for maintenance, etc
● Change in demand

Although it would not cause an overspending, a declining workload has the potential for built in savings which, if properly managed, would contribute to a better overall spending pattern. An example of this potential waste/savings can be observed in the case of the closure of Skegatilla Hospital. Originally the hospital was funded for the care of 72 patients at a cost of

£772000. When the patient numbers fell to 36, the cost would have remained at almost the same level unless efforts were made to reduce spending to a comparable level. This is particularly necessary since a smaller number of patients are likely to have an increased average cost per patient week.

5.8.3 Funding deficits

Funding deficits are one of the most serious problems confronting the NHS, further exaggerated by increasing demand for more and better care and treatment. One is inescapably drawn to the conclusion that the NHS cannot continue to provide services in the same way as in the past. This is not intended to imply that the patient should suffer but rather that other methods must be found to manage the service more efficiently.

Tidying and cosmetic approaches have largely been exhausted and the reality of living with fewer beds, places and sessions has to be faced. Skegatilla Hospital was the victim of funding deficits as well as changes in the balance of care. The following financial considerations provided irrefutable ammunition:

	£(000)
Non-recurring	
● The condition of the estate (immediate needs)	120
● Internal environment not suitable for replacement (medium term)	3500
Recurring	
● Savings from the bringing into use of spare or wasted accommodation in Killybodagh	50
● Savings from recruitment costs of maintaining adequate staffing levels	25
● Direct savings which could be made from the closure	300
Total	373

The rationalisation of hospital beds in Killybodagh makes good budgetary sense as long as environmental and demographic influences remain the same. If, however, the population of over-65s was expected to increase by 4000 with a proportionately larger increase in the over-75 age group, during the five year strategic planning period, then some alternative provision for the care of the elderly would have to be contemplated.

In the event, the funding deficit occurred, partly because of a cash limit shortfall and partly because of intended changes in the balance of care. Although money was being saved in the hospital sector, funds were at the same time being earmarked for a whole range of developments aimed at:

● Maintenance of elderly people in the community
● Prevention of disability and handicap
● Provision of day care, respite care and other community support
● Support for relatives and the voluntary care sector

These additional developments considerably softened the impact of the loss of beds caused by the closure of Skegatilla Hospital.

It is important therefore that when managers are subject to severe budgetary pressure, they are also familiar with the complete budget plan so that alternative resources can be easily identified and, where appropriate, accessed.

5.9   Conclusion

5.9.1   General

The main objective of budget systems is to control resources within defined limits through involvement of the budget holder in the:

● Planning cycle
● Agreement and achievement of objectives
● Maintenance of professional standards

However, relentless financial pressure necessitates continual review of the total environment. This can mean that managers who might otherwise conform with the criteria may find that their operation does not fit well into the total environment.

Therefore, despite high quality care, low costs and ability to live within budget, other factors may prejudice the continuation of a particular regime. This was in fact the case with Skegatilla Hospital, which had a reputation for high quality, progressive, care of the elderly as well as a good financial record.

Budget managers must therefore be aware of their 'vulnerability rating'. The following check list can help budget holders to assess whether their service is likely to be at risk in circumstances of financial restrictions.

5.9.2 Operational feasibility check list

1. Background
   - Original purpose $\Big\}$ Historical legacy
   - Changes in purpose
   - Location (support lines etc.)
   - Likely political interests
     Local population; press etc
     Special support groups
     Catchment GPs
     Union impact

2. Provision of service
   - Patients' origin/relatives' travel distance, time convenience
   - Quality; activity; position in balance of care
   - Competition – alternatives available etc

3. Staff
   - Morale
   - Turnover
   - Difficulty and cost of recruitment

4. Estate
   - Condition
   - Immediate and past demands
   - Suitability

5. Finance
   - Budget performance
   - Cost of service

5.9.3   Positive action plan for maintaining the service

This chapter has taken a hospital closure as an example of budget setting and management. It is important, though, that budgeting should be seen as one part of a positive action plan for maintaining and developing services.

While high quality performance does not guarantee that a service will survive, modern management techniques can ensure that management will give due recognition to quality as well as to cost.

It must be recognised that the positive action plan is not intended as a crisis or panic measure but must be a part of a ward/department/hospital strategy. The main ingredients are:

1. Quality
   - The regime is appropriate, compassionate and is compatible with the patient's dignity
   - It is accessible and can demonstrate an equitable balance between waiting lists, value for money and outcomes
   - It makes use of techniques which are valid and modern

2. Marketing
   - Recognise likely competition
   - Identify and cherish sources of goodwill and maintain high profile through:
       Individuals
       Groups
       Press
       Open days
   - Be ready to know how to mobilise opinion

3. Resource management
   - Maintain high morale
   - Ensure that estate is kept in good condition and is suitable for the purpose
   - Live within budget; keep costs low; but be able to gain access to the spending cycle

At Skegatilla, management maintained a passive profile and was content to let a high quality economic service speak for itself. It was also passive about the clearly finite life expectancy of the estate. The hospital's peripheral location and its lack of active support made it highly vulnerable, and, when the feasibility review took place, it was too late for a service maintenance plan to be activated.

6

Managing Clinical Activity
Josephine Plant

6.1 Issues

- Clinical activity
- Professional autonomy
- Clinical budgeting

6.1.1 Clinical activity

Clinical activity may be defined as those practices which are directly concerned with the diagnosis, treatment and care of a person presenting with presumed or actual morbidity, when these are carried out by an appropriate registered professional worker or those under their supervision. However, not all registered professional health care staff who are engaged in measures or activities intended to improve health care status are performing clinical activity. A dietician reviewing the nutritional values of the cooked vegetables supplied to in-patients is not engaged in a clinical activity, but when that dietician is advising a physician on the food requirements of a patient undergoing certain types of chemotherapy, that may be properly designated as 'clinical activity'.

- The essence of clinical activity, therefore, is not that it is oriented to health care *per se*, but that it is oriented to the health care of a particular individual

6.1.2 Professional autonomy

How can a broad policy decision taken by the health authority to increase the proportion of ENT cases who are from within the

84

district be implemented? What happens if the district community physician believes that on the basis of QALYS – quality adjusted life years – the cardiothoracic surgeons should reduce the number of coronary artery bypass operations? What can be the response of the organisation if a consultant consistently performs fewer operations per session than colleagues doing a similar list? How can a consultant who keeps patients waiting a long time in the outpatient department be approached? It is argued that, in respect of all the above problems, the organisation can do very little and that any attempt to act on these issues against the wish of the consultant would be a breach of clinical autonomy.

The theory behind professional autonomy is that the professional, having undertaken the approved course of study, demonstrated competence in the theory and practice of the profession, and being duly licensed to practise by the appropriate professional body, may then act as an independent practitioner in the relevant area of activity. In so doing, professionals accept legal and moral responsibility for their activity in relation to the client. In assuming this legal and moral responsibility for the service supplied, they also demand freedom to supply that service in the manner they deem fit.

It is important to understand that clinical autonomy has been seen by medical practitioners in the UK as a crucial value since the professionalisation of medicine and surgery during the 19th century. It is also a value that medical practitioners frequently see as being under threat or subject to encroachment by politicians, managers and other professions.

Clinical autonomy is a concept that other health professions have borrowed from medicine in order to protect the integrity of their own domains of clinical practice and also to boost the status of their own profession or aspiring profession. Some doctors, though not all, would question the claims made by other professions to clinical autonomy or at least their interpretation of it; and increasingly the claims made by doctors for clinical autonomy are being questioned. These disagreements and changes that may occur in the understanding of the concept of clinical autonomy do not invalidate it; on the contrary they serve as evidence that it remains a crucial concept.

● Professional autonomy for health care staff means, therefore, independence of action and responsibility for action when the activity in question belongs within the recognised domain of that profession

In the UK, consultant medical staff have claimed wider powers, in the name of professional autonomy, than are enjoyed by their peers in many other countries. They not only exercise their right to treat individuals as they deem appropriate, but also to decide which patients they will see and to allow interest in specific diseases to divert the nature of their practice away from the service they were originally appointed to provide – even into a direction which falls outside the goals of the health authority. This can cause considerable difficulties for the managers of the health authority who are charged with responsibility for broad policy matters and for ensuring that resources are used efficiently and effectively.

6.1.3   Clinical budgeting

Clinical budgeting may be seen as an intelligent response to the complex issues, problems and conflicts raised by clinical or professional autonomy under conditions where other groups claim either the right or the responsibility for determining health care resource allocation and the management of health care expenditure. These groups include government, civil servants, health managers, local interest lobbies, consumers etc. The introduction of clinical budgeting is an approach to the problem posed when the 'rational' but unfettered micro-decisions of individual autonomous clinicians might in total produce an 'irrational' macro allocation of resources.

Clinical budgeting says to the clinician, 'If you claim personal responsibility for your clinical practice you must then equally be prepared to accept ownership of the management and financial consequences of that position.' The stick behind this proposition is that government (supported by a more questioning public) is poised to 'take on' the medical profession and remove many of its legal privileges as a residual middle class monopoly. The carrot, however, is that if doctors were to get more directly involved in 'hands on' management with real general management power, then they would not only escape the irritation of centralised administration but receive the benefits of the extra efficiency and resources released by devolved and flexible management.

Clinical budgeting gets around the problem created by the hospital consultant view of clinical autonomy by saying to the clinical director, 'If Mr X imports all his patients from outside the district, if Dr Y is always late for outpatient appointments, if Mr Z won't ensure that adequate discharge arrangements are in place, then these are your problems. Even though you may not be able to force them to alter their ways, they are your peers and you can use your influence, introduce peer review and manipulate peer group pressure.'

● Clinical budgeting institutionalises and makes more explicit the financial and managerial responsibility of the clinical director and his team

Obtaining the agreement of the clinical director, the following may, for example, be negotiated:

1. Cash limits on the directorate.
2. Restrictions of the total number of certain operations per year.
3. The need to increase the proportion of district ENT cases.
4. To keep two different waiting lists – one for district residents and one for non district residents.

Arrangements to introduce clinical budgeting must ensure that each directorate has good financial and health activity data supplied for local management purposes. The 'centre' knows that its policies and goals are understood and accepted by the 'periphery'. It also knows that the directorates upon whom it depends to implement the policies actually own them. It thus integrates the centre with its periphery.

While clinical budgeting may at first sight appear to be solely concerned with maintaining financial discipline, its broader objective is to develop an organisational process that is capable of resolving the conflict between the imperative of management and the value of clinical autonomy.

6.2   Case study

St Luke's is a large teaching hospital which, in addition to providing a service to local residents, also has for some of its services a multi-district, regional and multi-regional catchment population, and will from time to time provide a facility of tertiary referral in most specialties.

Over the past few years, the health authority's policy of moving resources from hospital acute services to community care services has exacerbated the effects of reduction in resources resulting from the RAWP (Resource Allocation Working Party) arrangements. The managers of the acute hospital services have been facing increasingly difficult decisions, and health authority members have been placing greater emphasis on the provision of services to district residents as a priority for all services.

Nonetheless, if the institution is to retain its function as a teaching hospital, a balance between district and non-district patients must be maintained. Protective funding which regional services attract would be lost to the district *pro rata* to any reduction of those services. Reduction in these regional specialties would not, therefore, contribute to the required reduction in budget.

6.2.1   *The task for the surgical directorate*

The date for the budget review for the next financial year is approaching. The clinical director and his team of nurse and administrator have to plan general surgical activity for next year.

Team members are assisted by a named individual from the finance department and staff from the district information offices. The director of nursing services and the director of nurse education will give guidance and help to the nurse manager, and assistance and advice is available from the office of the general manager and the district medical officer. However each directorate is held accountable for achieving its plan and attaining its goals with the resources available.

6.2.2.   *Resources available to the team*

The five wards each have 25 beds and associated staff: one ward is devoted to urology; one ward does head and neck surgery and vascular surgery; three wards undertake general surgery.

6.2.3 Non-staff budgets

Such expenditure includes stationery, medical and surgical equipment, drugs, dressing etc.

6.2.4 Staff and departments influenced but not controlled by the directorate

These include non-clinical support staff, for example, cleaners, porters, maintenance workers and so on, together with clinical support staff such as those who work in X-ray, physiotherapy, occupational therapy and speech therapy.

6.2.5 Planning guidelines

1. To maintain the same level of the surgical activity, measured by the district in-house performance indicators, as in the previous year, while increasing the proportion of district residents treated by 10 per cent.
2. A requirement to take a 1 per cent cut on the previous year's budget.
3. To improve the effectiveness of planning for patients being discharged home from hospital.
4. To reduce time between a referral letter being received from a general practitioner and the first clinic appointment for that patient to see a consultant.
5. To reduce the time spent by patients waiting in the out-patient department to be seen.
6. To maintain their known commitment to basic and postbasic nurse education.
7. To improve the quality of the care provided in the surgical directorate.

The directorate and the district management board have negotiated these guidelines and policy objectives. They are understood and accepted.

6.3   Problems and solutions

In pulling together the facts relating to the past performance of the surgical services, the three fulltime members of the team will bring to their task of compiling the service plan for the next year considerable personal observation, ideas from staff working in the directorate and opinions from unit and district officers. There will also be comparative data gleaned from studying performance indicators. As colleagues working together on a daily basis, they can each challenge the assumptions and prejudices of the other and together contemplate the 'unthinkable'.

In their efforts to protect the provision of patient services at the maximum possible level, the director and his team will review all expenditure heads within the directorate (including overhead costs, semi-variable costs and variable costs) to ensure that money is not wasted by lack of attention to detail by any manager.

6.3.1   *Overhead costs*

These are the costs which are not controlled by the team and may include such items as rates, heating and lighting and also the costs of some district-provided services such as laundry and CSSD. Over the year the members of the clinical team will wish to know about the constituent parts of overhead costs to:

● Determine whether they appear to be reasonable
● Determine whether the directorate is getting value for money from services subsumed within them
● To challenge them and influence the level at which they are set

If the costs of the laundry service, for example, seem unduly high and the service, from the point of view of the internal consumer (wards and departments), is in some way unsatisfactory then other directorate teams are likely to hold similar views. They may ask the district management team to review the service in order to reduce the overhead costs charged to the directorate and to improve the service. The quality and quantity of support services are integral to the management of clinical services and as such are a proper area of concern for clinical managers. When requesting a review of support services, facts will be more compelling than opinions:

- How often over the past six months or year have wards or departments had insufficient linen, CSSD, portering services, patient meals arriving at temperatures outside those required by food and hygiene regulations etc.?
- Was there a discernable pattern to these inadequacies?

The costs of clinical services should also be reviewed. The directorate is charged for its use of theatres on the basis of booked sessions. It is therefore important to discover if all sessions are fully utilised and investigate reasons if that is not the case. If a session habitually starts late because key staff do not arrive on time, it may be that:

- Those sessions need rescheduling
- Ward rounds or outpatient sessions need rescheduling

If sessions habitually start on time but overrun, thus carrying the cost of enhanced hours or overtime payments for nurses, different considerations arise:

- Discuss with the surgeon arranging the list the reality of his expectation about operation times
- Are too many emergencies arising which have to be fitted into normal lists? Is some rescheduling possible?
- Is the service 'overbedded' for the available theatre time?

Similar questions arise in relation to the use of other clinical service departments and similar action may be found appropriate.

Moreover, the nurse manager will need to review with ward staff their ordering and use of:

- Packs from central sterile supply (CSSD)
- Linen
- Patients' meals

- Ward stocks of medical and surgical equipment
- Ward stocks of stationery

Over a relatively short period of a month or so, it is not unknown for the number of patients' meals ordered for a small group of wards to exceed the number of patients by a number well into three figures. It is also well known that, in some wards, stockpiles of equipment may be found which are far in excess of their likely usage over a reasonable timescale. Such over ordering may represent quite significant expenditure charges to the ward and thus to the directorate.

6.3.2   Semi variable costs

These are the costs which are influenced and affected by the team but there is usually a longer timescale before decisions made by the team can be seen to have an effect on these costs. For example, a decision by the surgical directorate to reduce significantly the number of X-rays ordered will have the effect of decreasing the workload of the X-ray department. The decreased demand on the department may well be sufficient to enable them to reduce their staffing establishment. This reduction in staffing is likely to occur over a period of several months and the savings which may be realised will probably not result in any financial adjustments until the next financial year.

6.3.3   Variable costs

These are the costs which bear a direct relationship to the volume of patient activity, such as expenditure on drugs.

Many districts positively encourage the use of less expensive drugs where the clinical effect is not significantly different from that produced by more expensive preparations. Analysis of drug use will be greatly facilitated by the involvement of the district pharmacist.

Attempts to monitor the doctors and their working routines may be seen as threatening clinical autonomy and will require tact and discretion if there is to be a positive outcome. It is in the resolution of problems such as these that the clinical director may provide the invaluable mechanism of exerting peer group pressure, though he may also need to find 'savings' from the directorate budget to enable him to offer the 'carrot' of the ability to buy that rather expensive new piece of equipment!

6.4 Compiling the service plan for next year

6.4.1 *The balance between district and non-district patients*

Each 'firm' within the directorate is asked to produce a mini business programme outlining the next year's clinical workload and how it fits into the various policy constraints. These mini business programmes rely on clinicians' knowledge of their waiting lists, including the numbers of district and non-district patients.

The clinical director chairs a series of meetings with the surgeons using historical data provided by the administrator and taking into account the nursing viewpoint on manageable workloads.

It is agreed after much discussion and some 'horse trading' that the bulk of the increase in district cases will result from more elective surgery by the urologists who will have a 'blitz' on the district's waiting lists. During these discussions the urologists make some pointed comments about the work of the general surgeons. The discussion also raises the question about the use of beds and the fall in occupancy at weekends in some wards. Further analysis of data may produce an opportunity to make inroads on the required 1 per cent budget reduction.

6.4.2 *Planning to achieve the budget reduction*
The district information officer will be able to supply information on annual average bed use, together with selected information on a rolling programme basis updated periodically throughout the year and relating to:

● The number of available beds
● The number of occupied beds
● The turnover interval
● Case mix
● The length of stay by diagnostic related groups

Analysis over a 5 year period has shown a significant increase in the caseload. More detailed investigation highlights that the throughput of patients in each available bed has risen from 30.1 to 32.7 per annum, the length of stay has decreased from 10.1 days to 9.4 days and the turnover interval has reduced from 2.2 days to 1.8 days. Thus it may be initially concluded that efficiency has improved over this time period according to one rough set of measures. However, the finance officer says that the apparent improvements fail to reflect the extra cost of the additional registrar and nurses employed in this period.

Performance indicators can provide considerable help in comparing the performance in one district in relation to other districts, but care is needed in their interpretation and in deciding which conclusions may appropriately be drawn. After the best batch of performance indicators has been selected, it will be helpful to obtain comparisons with similar institutions.

In the particular instance of a surgical unit in a teaching hospital one may wish to see the comparisons with:

● All London teaching hospitals
● All teaching hospitals in England
● Any other grouping which may seem relevant

More specific questions can then be posed as to why the performance of this service differs from that of an apparently similar service in a comparable authority. If no difference is elicited which would satisfactorily explain the difference in the performance indicators then further discussion may highlight other ways of providing the services to improve performance.

In the event, the report indicates that the length of stay is shorter than that for comparable services in other districts but that the ratio of nurses to patients is higher than average. This is partially explained by the case mix and the greater dependency of patients in the regional specialty wards.

The nurse manager agrees that though staffing appears appropriate to the workload during the week, at weekends nursing staff are not well utilised and this may well explain the apparent high nursing ratios. None the less it is proposed that because the nurses are 'overworked' during the week, they deserve a more relaxed pace at the weekends, and also need that time to catch up on the educational needs of the nurses in training.

A scrutiny of inpatient statistics ward by ward may reveal that a specialist ward such as that devoted to head and neck surgery with vascular surgery has a high occupancy spread evenly over the week, and despite a high proportion of patients being very nurse dependent most days, the nursing establishment is lower than in the remaining wards. The reason is that the sister and consultants work closely together in managing admissions and caseload. Their proportion of emergency admissions to planned admissions is low.

In an effort to introduce a similar level of predictability to the work in the remaining wards, it may be possible to concentrate emergency admissions for all surgeons into one ward only, or to arrange a weekly rotation for wards to take emergency admissions. The week scheduled for the emergency admissions should be a week in which there are no planned admissions.

Further study of the number of day cases, and the average length of stay may enable the use of another ward for day care only, or perhaps conversion to a 5 day ward. The possible savings on nurses no longer required to work at weekends or on night duty on one or two wards will make a major contribution to the 1 per cent budget reduction. These types of changes will require careful planning and monitoring if there is not to be an unintended and undesired change of case mix in the directorate. They will also require a careful reappraisal of the staffing requirements and consultation with the school of nursing concerning the learner experience which they could offer.

The finance officer allocated to the surgical directorate undertakes to provide projected costings for this proposed change in service delivery and throughout the year will provide detailed expenditure statements on a monthly basis to enable the team to establish at an early point in the financial year any undesirable trends in expenditure.

Staffing in all grades and disciplines in the service will be reviewed by the directorate team. However, the largest single group will be nurses, and it will be this group which attracts the most attention.

For many doctors, the introduction of clinical budgeting heralds a major culture shock when they discover how many nurses are employed, and that about six whole time equivalent nurses are needed on the payroll in order to produce one nurse on duty for a 24-hour period 365 days a year. Their first reaction is that there are far too many and that the resources devoted to the nursing services may therefore be significantly reduced, or that a more flexible deployment of the same number of nurses may improve the quality of care. They may be right; it is therefore important to listen to what they have to say. This is when the nurse manager must be able to account to non-nurses for decisions based on professional knowledge, experience and judgement, using quantitative demonstrations wherever possible.

There are many ways of calculating the number of nurses required to work in a particular ward. Clinical budgeting processes lend themselves more easily to the bottom up approach – of which there are many forms. Mostly, however, they attempt to take account of the workload generated by patients in beds and for that reason are more likely to produce an acceptable result than top down methods which assume a bed to be a standard entity in workload terms.

The requirement for nurse staffing in any clinical situation is influenced by several factors:

● The need for knowledge, skill and nurses on duty to care for the normal patient case mix in any particular ward
● The degree to which the work is predictable – how many patients are planned 'cold' admissions and how many arrive as emergency admissions
● The adequacy of support services – how much skilled nursing time is expended plugging gaps left by inadequate support services?
● The quality of care deemed acceptable. A high proportion of patients in most wards tend to be elderly, and the decision must be made by the clinical director and his team as to whether they recommend in their business programme that sufficient staff will be allocated to promote a vigorous and active rehabilitation programme or whether a more laissez-faire or custodial kind of care is accepted as the only standard which can be afforded

If they decide that they cannot afford active rehabilitation, they will explain in their business programme the consequences of that decision in terms of the effects of institutionalisation, increased demand for continuing care places and reduced QALYS. It may be that the general manager at unit or district level, or indeed the health authority itself will deem quality to be more important than quantity and instruct the directorate to rethink the issue:

● The extent to which the ward sister or charge nurse is actively consulted over the capacity of the ward and its admissions and discharge policies. This consultation or lack of it may affect the level of agency, bank and overtime working
● The care that has been taken to ensure that predictable weekly variations in workload are reflected in staff rostering
● The extent to which the pattern of the inpatient day can be adjusted to the benefit of both patients and staff rostering
● The extent to which nurse education at basic, postbasic and in-service levels impinge on the staffing required

6.4.3   *Planned discharge arrangements*

Ideally, plans for going home from hospital should start before admission, and certainly no later than the day of admission.

● Friends, relatives and neighbours who are willing to ensure that the home is clean and warm, and that a few days' supply of food has been obtained ready for the patient's homecoming, will need notice of the expected date of discharge
● Social services such as home helps or meals on wheels often require several days' notice before they can start their services
● General practitioners and district nurses are more likely to be quickly responsive to a call from the patient if they have had prior notice about what has happened in hospital and when to expect the patient home
● A domiciliary assessment visit before discharge from hospital by an occupational therapist or appropriate professional worker will help to ensure that any aids to mobility and daily living will be available when needed

It is agreed that a smooth transition from hospital to home is part of good patient care. It is also generally accepted that the final responsibility for adequate discharge planning rests with the consultant. However, custom and practice usually means that the coordination of plans is delegated to the ward sister. A *pro forma* is designed to assist in overcoming the problems of rapid staff turnover and the need for continuous training. It will be used by doctors, nurses, social workers and therapists who will indicate by means of a date and signature those discharge arrangements which have been satisfactorily organised.

6.4.4　*Reduction of the waiting time for the first outpatient appointment*

The time taken for a referral letter from a general practitioner to go through the public postal system is outside the control of the surgical directorate. They therefore concentrate on:

1. Reducing the time between receipt of the letter in the hospital and the despatch of the clinic appointment to the patient.
2. Reducing the time lapse between receipt of the referral letter and the date of the first appointment.

Possible solutions to these problems are not difficult or complex, but politically they may prove very problematic as there are almost as many ways of 'managing the waiting list' as there are consultants attempting to do so. Some allow the entire process to be undertaken by clerical staff in the outpatient department, others delegate to a 'junior doctor' and yet others deal with all referral letters personally.

The clinical director with his team formulate proposals, but it will then be largely the director, using peer group pressure, who will persuade and cajole his colleagues to change. His approach in talking to his colleagues will be to agree with each of them a reasonable standard time for 1 and 2, taking into account what each feels to be possible. Perhaps something between two and five working days to despatch the appointment may be reasonable. Then for appointments arranged, standards agreed might be 'next clinic' for urgent referrals, within three weeks for non urgent district residents and six to eight weeks for the rest.

They then need to devise the quality assurance procedure

which, if followed, will ensure that those standards are normally met, and agree a system of quality control which will monitor that the standards are normally achieved. In year one, different consultants in the directorate may define different standards which can then be reviewed periodically. If the consultants are to be persuaded to review the quality of their services, it is important that they individually agree the standard set for their part of the service. In this way their sense of 'ownership' for the standard is enhanced. It also helps to ensure that they view the standard as achievable.

In order to improve the use of clinic time, and to create appointment times for new patients, the administrator is asked to review all outpatients, discussing his findings with the appropriate consultant and seeking the advice of the director as needed.

- He will ensure that all surgical referral letters arrive on the desk of the appropriate surgeon within 24 hours of receipt in the hospital
- He may write to the GPs of the patients who have been waiting for a first appointment for a period of several weeks to discover if they still need that appointment
- He will undertake a comparative analysis using performance indicators to raise questions on the ratio of 'new' to 'follow-up' patients, the objective being to reduce the follow-up visits and thus free appointments for new patients. This will be an area seen to impinge on clinical autonomy and for that reason, it will probably be the clinical director who uses the analysis to open discussions with his colleagues. It may be agreed that this review will be undertaken routinely every six months

6.4.5 *Waiting time in the clinic*

To achieve a reduction in waiting time, a similar exercise involving agreeing standards, instituting quality assurance and quality control mechanisms will be necessary.

Most people would agree that a reasonable standard would state that outpatients in a clinic should have been seen by their doctor within half an hour of their stated time of appointment. Repeated failure to meet the agreed standard may arise for a number of reasons. However, clinical management gives the responsibility to the director and his team to investigate the cause, find a solution and implement a more effective system.

- Does the clinic need rescheduling, either to a time when the medical staff can guarantee their availability or to allow nurses and other staff sufficient time to set up specialist equipment?
- Is the booking system appropriate to the specialty? Some specialities need longer consultation times than others and first appointments need more time than follow-up visits. One of the advantages of devolving clinical management to a point as close as possible to those engaged in clinical activity is that the people making these decisions are the ones who fully understand the requirements of their services

6.5   Issues and concluding observations

In asking the questions, defining the problems and proposing solutions, the surgical directorate will arrive at the production of its service plan for the next year, and will within that plan ensure that the guidelines and policy objectives are addressed. Nonetheless, for the management of clinical activity and for budgetary responsibility to be successfully devolved to clinical teams of doctors, nurses and administrators, not only must the members of the team be willing and able to accept that responsibility but the district officers and the health authority must also play their part:

- They must be prepared to offer to those providing the services as much autonomy and flexibility as is possible in a public service
- They must provide accurate information on expenditure and activity to enable and encourage departments, directorates and clinical teams to monitor and find ways of improving the services they offer

For managers working at the centre of an organisation, be it at unit or district level, there are problems.

1. It was always difficult to communicate effectively with all staff even when there were clear functional lines of management. The problem of disseminating information on organisational goals, professional standards, organisational imperatives is exacerbated by the need to communicate effectively with each directorate and to ensure that the team communicates with the staff working there. Mechanisms such as newsletters and team briefings have proved helpful.
2. Tensions may develop between directorates and the unit or district level. Some organisational tension is healthy – too much is not! Effective guidelines for the preparation of service plans, and clear agreed lines of professional accountability help to reduce the likelihood of destructive tension, as also does the availability and willingness of unit and district managers to meet clinical directors and their teams to talk through problems.
3. There is an increased problem of planning across services. Any directorate may make decisions which seem perfectly rational within that service, without pausing to consider the likely impact on other services.
4. The problem of inconsistent strengths or performance by individual directorates is difficult but perhaps self limiting as more managers become used to accepting responsibility for problem solving and the resultant action plan. Appropriate management training is helpful in speeding up the learning process.

The strengths of managing clinical activity by devolving management responsibility and budgets to clinical teams as described are:

1. The promotion of creativity and innovation at the clinical level by those with the most detailed knowledge of the requirements of their particular services. Within the team, each head of service is responsible to the director for the management and provision of their part of the service. The director coordinates their efforts to ensure that they are all directed towards the achievement of their common goal.

2. That it facilitates responsiveness to consumer views and a changing environment. New knowledge, new techniques and clinical regimes can gain a rapid response from a management team operating so close to the patient.
3. That it fosters collaboration between doctors, nurses, administrators and finance officers because, being so close to the point of service delivery, all can see the need for team work to improve patient care.
4. Close collaboration and regular meetings between team members reduces decision-making time, and having worked closely together to produce their plan, all are enthusiastic to focus on, and monitor the outcome.

Bibliography

N. Bosanquet, 'Outpatient Services – a case for treatment', *Health Service Journal*, **97**, No. 5050 (1987) pp. 550–1

R. Coxford, 'Pressure is on to deliver the goods', *Health Service Journal*, **96**, No. 5023 (1986) p. 1426.

Draft Circular on Discharge of Patients From Hospital (London: DHSS 1988).

M. Fairey, *Information Management in the Hospital and Community Health Services. Guidance for Information Strategies* (London: Information Management Group, 1987).

C. Gudex, *QUALYS and Their Use By the Health Service* (Centre for Health Economics, University of York, 1986).

M. Harley and J. Yates, 'Performance Indicators in the Health Service', *Public Finance and Accounting* (6 November 1987) pp. 9–12.

J. Harris, 'Qualifying the value of life', *Journal of Medical Ethics*, **13**, No. 3 (1987) pp. 117–123.

J. Holmgren and W. Wentz, *Material Management and Purchasing for the Health Care Facility* (Aupha Press, 1982).

L. Jenkins, M. Bardsley, J. Coles, I. Wickings and H. Leow, *Use and Validity of NHS Performance Indicators – A National Survey* (King Edward's Hospital Fund for London, 1987).

T. Jones and M. Prowle, *Health Service Finance. An Introduction* (CAET, 1987).

M. Jupp, 'Going Home', *Nursing Times*, **82**, No. 40 (1986) pp. 40–2; **85**, No. 1 (1988) pp. 23–4.

K. D. Lafferty, 'Patient Care Systems, vs Financial Systems: the cost justification battle, *Nursing Management* **18**, No. 7 (1987) pp. 51–5.

A. F. Long and S. Harrison (eds), *Health Services Performance* (Lone Croom Helm, 1985).

A. Mason and V. Morrison, *Walk, Don't Run. A Collection of Essays on Information Issues* (King Edward's Hospital Fund for London, 1985).

Nurse Manpower: Maintaining the Balance (London: DHSS, 1982).

A. Pearson, *Nursing Quality Measurement. Quality Assurance Methods for Peer Review* (Chichester: Wiley, 1987).

Performance Indicators for the NHS (London: DHSS, 1982).

J. Perrin, *Resource Management in the NHS* (Wokingham: Van Nostrand Reinhold, 1988).

J. P. Sweeney and A. Mason, 'Integrated Hospital Information Systems', *Journal of the Royal College Physicians London* **21**, No. 2 (1987) pp. 102–4.

ging the Quality of

Alison Kitson

7.1 Introduction

Quality assurance in health care is about making sure that the service is being provided to a level that has been defined according to pre-determined criteria and standards. A major problem, however, is that often these standards do not exist and if they do they are frequently written in ways that make them very difficult to measure.

A lot of work has been done to define the quality of the environment where people work and where patients are treated. These descriptions can sometimes be used as environmental or structure standards, but so far little has been done in the United Kingdom to agree standards about the interventions of practitioners, that is to say, how they should go about the job and what they are hoping to achieve.

Because of this, managers find themselves in a difficult situation. They are supposed to be able to measure the quality of the service and initiate improvement plans if the service is not meeting the agreed standards. If standards do not exist, then this is a difficult task. If imprecise and out-of-date standards exist, this too creates other problems. If the workers – the clinicians, carers and support services – do not see the need for such statements, an additional problem confronts the manager – how to get people to see the need for regular evaluation and review of the service being delivered to patients.

Assuring the quality of the service, then, would seem to be everybody's business but each group of workers has a different part to play:

● Someone has to set the target and define what quality is. Is quality about treating patients as people or is it about reducing the waiting list or is it about both?
● Someone else has to sort out the standards
● Others have to be involved in the review mechanisms
● And still others have to keep the whole system going

Introducing quality assurance to a unit or hospital does require careful co-ordination and planning and is best achieved with the help of personnel appropriately trained in quality assurance techniques who can be used as resource persons by the manager.

7.2 The case study

Mrs Smith had several years' experience behind her as a director of nursing services of a neighbouring hospital for the care of the elderly when she accepted the post of service manager of care for the elderly services in District X. She was looking forward to her new job, encompassing as it did the overall co-ordination and running of all the services within the elderly care unit. She had been impressed at interview by reports of the dynamic approach adopted to patient care by the multidisciplinary team and was looking forward to seeing how the large rehabilitation unit actually catered for the different therapeutic needs of long stay, rehabilitation, assessment and day care patients.

The upper storey of the purpose built unit comprised four 30-bed wards for mixed assessment, rehabilitation and some long stay patients waiting for placement. The ground floor housed the day hospital and the therapy units used primarily by the physiotherapy, occupational therapy and speech therapy staff. The unit had its own ancillary and catering staff. The nursing and medical staff had moved from the old hospital when the new unit had been opened three years previously.

It was not too long before Mrs Smith discovered that all was not as it had appeared at her interview. The dynamic approach to patient care turned out to be a description for the frantic activity that took place every weekday morning to try and get as many patients from the wards to therapy as possible. On questioning the ward sisters as to why the patients were going, the reply came that it was what the physiotherapy department wanted. On questioning the paramedical staff, the reason was perceived in terms of overall therapeutic patient goals and in line with the dynamic approach. On questioning the medical staff, the response was that it had all been discussed at the multidisciplinary meetings.

What Mrs Smith perceived from each of the groups she spoke to was a lack of shared understanding of the purpose and objectives of the dynamic approach. She also uncovered a lot of resentment from certain groups of staff in having to meet the demands of other groups of workers, particularly the resentment of nursing staff at having to prepare patients for therapy which, in their opinion, was not very beneficial.

The underlying tension came to a head following a complaint from the daughter of one of the rehabilitation patients. Apparently the patient in question had been left unattended in a wheelchair while the porter had gone to fetch another patient from the therapy department. The patient (Mrs Matthews) had somehow fallen out of the chair and had sustained a large bump on her head. When her daughter visited that evening Mrs Matthews burst into tears and told her how she hated the unit, the treatment and the perpetual rush everyone seemed to be in. Mrs Matthews' daughter was married to a health authority member.

The letter of complaint had been sent to the district general manager who passed it to the quality assurance officer. The quality assurance officer arranged a meeting with Mrs Smith to discuss the matter. Both the quality assurance officer and Mrs Smith realised the complexity of the problem and spent most of their first meeting together debating whether to respond to the obvious problem by increasing the number of portering staff or to actually confront the situation and try and find a more lasting solution.

The quality assurance officer said that he would deal with the letter and would act as a resource to Mrs Smith but that it was up to her to decide how she was going to improve the situation. He also said that the district general manager wanted a full report of the situation within six months together with evidence that the service had improved.

7.3 Problems and solutions

7.3.1 *The plan*

The first thing Mrs Smith did following her meeting with the quality assurance officer was to call a meeting of the chief paramedical staff, the consultants, and the nursing officers for the day hospital and wards. The meeting was a disaster – the chief physiotherapist and one of the senior nurses just could not communicate with each other and it was clear that resentment had built up on either side to such a degree that any attempt at dialogue and identification of the underlying problem was going to be very difficult. Somehow the stalemate had to be broken and the various groups helped to communicate with each other.

While the complaint had brought the situation to a head, Mrs Smith discovered that there was no precise information available in the records about the daily movement of patients from the wards to the therapy units. Thus she was not able to tell whether the incident involving Mrs Matthews had been an exception or whether it was reflecting the system stretched to the limit. Priority number one was to obtain some baseline information on how the system was working and priority number two was to try and build up more positive communication between the members of the multidisciplinary team.

The quality assurance officer believed Mrs Smith could take one of three possible approaches to solving her problem:

1. She could implement an audit and obtain a picture of the overall working of the department.
2. She could arrange a number of informal group meetings to discuss the situation.
3. She could set up a 'task group' that would be charged with coming up with a solution to the problem. This could either take the form of a quality circle or it could be seen as a standard setting group.

After careful reflection Mrs Smith decided to go for the formation of a standard setting group. While a formal audit would have shown up a range of issues which staff were denying, Mrs Smith believed that this would be an inappropriate method to use in the circumstances, given the mistrust and defensiveness she detected between certain staff members. A method which provided information and also helped people to explore their own attitudes and work methods was necessary. However, it had to be structured with clearly defined parameters and a strong leader. This ruled out the informal group meetings and left her with option three.

The standard setting group method was selected in preference to the quality circle approach for two reasons. One was that the standard setting group method introduced groups of practitioners to standard setting and criteria formulation through solving clinical problems. Thus groups using this method would not only find solutions to problems but would also develop criteria sets and agree standards which could then be used to evaluate performance over time. The other – more pragmatic – reason was that the quality assurance officer said he knew more about the dynamic standard setting approach than quality circles and as he had offered to facilitate the group Mrs Smith was prepared to give it a try.

7.3.2   The progress

A second meeting was arranged for the heads of the unit to meet with the quality assurance officer and Mrs Smith. This time Mrs Smith took a much more directive role, shared her impressions of the situation with the group, outlined her concerns and then presented the draft plan of action which outlined how the standard setting group would be constituted, what it would have to do and how long it would have to do it.

Basically what she told them was that the present group of head physiotherapist, occupational therapist, speech therapist, two consultants, and two senior nurses would comprise the coordinating group whose job would be to receive and act on the information provided by colleagues who were more directly involved in the day-to-day running of the service. Each member of the coordinating group was to identify a person who would be willing to work in the standard setting group over the next six months or until the resolution of the problem. Thus it had to be made clear that the heads of the unit were entrusting the analysis of the situation and the possible resolution of it to more locally based workers. The quality assurance officer explained that this was a very important part to the whole concept of quality improvement – ownership and participation in problem-solving and standard setting helped to commit people to common goals and objectives.

There were of course a few cynics in the group who said it was a waste of time and that they could not see their colleagues wanting to be part of such proceedings. After all, the quality of the service was the responsibility of every practitioner and if they could not assure it then they should not be practising.

All the heads of the unit save one of the consultants agreed to discuss the plan with their colleagues and nominate one person to serve on the standard setting group. Three weeks later the first meeting of the standard setting group was held. The group comprised the ward sister from each of the four wards; a registered nurse from the day unit, two physiotherapists, one occupational therapist, one registrar, and one senior house officer. The quality assurance officer attended the first meeting and outlined the following steps in the standard setting process:

- Defining the problem
- Collecting baseline information
- Agreeing norms for the service
- Formulating criteria
- Refining criteria
- Agreeing standard statement
- Setting review date
- Monitoring activity
- Evaluating results
- Devising action plan

He also described the role of the coordinating group which would be responding to the information produced by the standard setting group. The group then sorted out how often, how long and where it would meet. The quality assurance officer agreed to come to the meetings to act as facilitator and the group selected one of the physiotherapists as its leader. Everyone did admit to being slightly dubious about the whole process and some even admitted to being sceptical about whether it could really change the situation.

7.3.3   *The activity*

Over the next three months the group met for one and a half hours every two weeks during work hours. An average of six people plus the quality assurance officer attended the meetings which became very lively after the initial introductory meeting. The group started out by trying to agree a common interpretation of the problem. This was difficult as they discovered each discipline had a different way of looking at the situation. One technique which helped the group was to undertake a 12-hour critical incidence study where two members volunteered to observe the flow of patients coming into and out of the therapy departments. Their information on the throughput and impressions of the interactions was then related to a review of a sample of ten patients' case notes.

From the observations and the chart review the standard setting group identified a number of major problem areas:

● Inconsistency in treatment of patients classified under similar dependency headings
● No common goals set for patient rehabilitation programmes by members of the multidisciplinary team
● Evaluation dates not set
● Rehabilitation programmes not discussed routinely at MDT meetings
● Confusion over certain policies relating to provision of portering services
● Selection of patients to attend for therapy was unclear
● Staff unclear as to overall objectives of therapy
● Patients' wishes and opinions did not seem to be taken into account
● Coordination of other services, e.g. catering, cleaning, and portering, with therapeutic services was poor

From this baseline information they then set about discussing what sort of services they should be providing. The provisional set of criteria and the summary standard statement with the review date were formulated and sent to the coordinating group for comments.

7.4   The first review meetings

Mrs Smith took the chair at the coordinating group meeting and circulated the preliminary report that had been drawn up by the standard setting group. The background paper outlined the key problem areas, and the provisional standard summarized the criteria which the group had devised as a first step towards evaluating the quality of the service (Figure 7.1). To begin with the response of the coordinating group to the information was cautious. While no-one could reject the analysis of the problem it was quite another matter to give assent to the statements embodied in the criteria. A number of quite radical changes were being suggested and some group members were not convinced that this was necessary.

The standard setting group leader, Jane Bradshaw, had been invited to present the group's work and, sensing the hesitancy of the coordinating group to respond to the information, she began to outline a number of changes that were already happening as a result of their work. For example, following the realisation that some form of joint assessment of patients' actual and potential level of independence had to be undertaken, three of the group had agreed to go away and review a range of approaches, discuss the logistics with staff and report back to the group. Another group member volunteered to look at the possibility of drafting the unit philosophy and he had already elicited the support of two other colleagues. The whole question of the 'health' of the multidisciplinary team meetings had also been raised and the registrar had agreed to have a look at this.

Jane went on to explain that each of these areas had to be addressed if they were to meet the criteria which they had set. She also reminded the coordinating group that it was their job to review the criteria in terms of desirability and achievability and that if they believed that adherence to them would reflect an acceptable quality of service, then it was everyone's duty to try and work towards their achievement.

At this point Mrs Smith added that as service manager it was her ultimate responsibility to ensure that the service being provided was both the most effective and most efficient she could achieve and that she would like some information on the criteria comparing lengths of treatment and types of therapy.

Figure 7.1   Provisional standard for evaluation
Topic: Therapeutic regimens for patients in rehabilitation unit
Standard Statement: Every patient will have an individual rehabilitation
   programme drawn up in conjunction with the key nurse and paramedical staff
Criteria:

Structure	Process	Outcome
1. The unit policy on rehabilitation creates the expectation that patients' individual needs and wishes are taken into account in the planning of therapy. 2. Patients' therapeutic regimens are drawn up taking into account the supply of catering, portering, cleaning and other ancillary services in the unit. 3. All staff working in the unit will be given a copy of the unit philosophy. 4. Unit policies pertaining to the provision of therapy will be reviewed by named practitioners within pre-set time limits.	1. The key nurse and named paramedical staff assess each patients' actual and potential level of independence within 48 hours of admission to the unit. 2. The key nurse and named paramedical staff in conjunction with the patient draw up a therapeutic plan identifying achievable targets and review dates. 3. The key nurse and named medical and paramedical staff set the first evaluation date following the assessment and record it in the patient's notes. 4. The multidisciplinary team uses a problem-solving approach to patient care and records information on same notes.	1. The patient will achieve the predicted level of independence in mobility activities within the specified time. 2. The patient will achieve the predicted level of independence in self-care activities within the specified time. 3. The patient reports satisfaction with the therapeutic regimen. 4. The patients' relatives/carers report satisfaction with the therapeutic regimen.

For example, she wondered whether the standard setting group
had discussed the idea of introducing teaching sessions on self-
medication and healthy living as a part of the therapeutic plan.
Such sessions could also be extended to carers to ensure that
the necessary preventive health care knowledge was being communicated effectively. Also she could see no reason why thera-

peutic plans ought not to include local trips to shopping centres, or to the pub so that therapy staff could assess more accurately the recovery and level of self-confidence of patients.

These points were duly noted by Jane who was then asked about the measurability of some of the criteria. One member of the group was particularly worried about the outcome criteria. He felt they were not discrete enough and would be impossible to evaluate precisely. Jane replied that the group had experienced great difficulty in devising relevant outcome criteria and at this stage they could not improve them until they had completed the first evaluation. However, she did believe that they had made explicit a number of criteria that the majority of practitioners used routinely to evaluate their own performance. By writing them in this way every member of the multidisciplinary team would be able to discuss what their contribution had been to patient progress. And this was possible because the process and structure criteria identified who should be involved in the assessment and planning of the patients' therapeutic regimens.

Jane was then asked about how the group intended to monitor and evaluate whether the criteria were being met. She said that they had thought of selecting the next three admissions on each of the four wards and would introduce the joint assessment and planning approach. They proposed to follow these 12 patients through their rehabilitation programmes, comparing the progress of patients with individualised rehabilitation programmes with other patients in the ward. This would be done on an ongoing informal basis until they could devise a more precise checklist. They also reckoned it would take about 12 weeks to gather sufficient data to make any sort of evaluation.

The coordinating group decided to accept the criteria and standard statement as presented. The chairman noted the reservations of some of the members regarding the outcome criteria and agreed to raise this question after the first evaluation. The review date was set for six months' time when the standard setting group would be required to present the results of their first evaluation together with any necessary action plans. A major concern shared by the group was the scale of the task and the need for careful coordination and support for the standard setting group.

After the meeting Mrs Smith saw the quality assurance officer and reported the outcome. She said she was very pleased with the amount of activity that had been generated in such a short time and already she could see old prejudices beginning to be broken down. However, she was concerned that the standard setting group had omitted to include any of the ancillary staff in the proceedings and this was something which might cause problems, particularly when the group began to look at policies related to the ancillary and therapeutic services. She also was concerned that, three months on, she had no 'hard facts' for the district general manager and neither would she have a report ready for him in the six-month deadline he had requested. What she could do, however, was to send a summary of the coordinating group meeting, with a copy of the criteria and standards, and outline the next six months' activity. The quality assurance officer felt this would be acceptable.

7.5 General principles

Mrs Smith had taken advantage of an incident to investigate a much more complex problem that was affecting the quality of the service. With the expert help of the quality assurance officer she was able to set up a 'task force' at local level to identify the major issues and devise criteria against which performance would be measured. The activity of the local group had to be sanctioned by the professional heads of the unit and this second, and in some ways more difficult, group comprised the coordinating group. As her experience from the first meeting of the coordinating group confirmed, it was vital that any exercise undertaken had to be well organised, structured and facilitated by someone trained in small group techniques with detailed understanding of quality assurance methods. Her job as general facilitator and support person was much simpler because she could rely on the expert help of the quality assurance officer.

However, there was no time in the proceedings when she was not aware that the ultimate responsibility for the quality of the service rested on her shoulders; if the groups failed to come up with workable solutions, if they rejected the approach, or, if she found herself arbitrating in an interprofessional squabble, then she was the person responsible for finding the solution. The three months' experience with the groups had helped to show her how quality assurance fitted in to the general management of the unit and the skills of problem identification, criteria formulation and evaluation of practice were very valuable, particularly in a multidisciplinary setting. What encouraged her most was the fact that the approach had helped staff to look at a problem in a constructive and patient focused way. And despite the few grumblings, she felt that the amount and quality of communication between staff had improved as a result.

She did, however, have a number of fears. First, what would she do if the results of the evaluation showed no improvements in patient care? Second, what would happen to the groups if the quality assurance officer could not support them? Third, how was she going to sustain the interest in the system? And, fourth, how was she going to involve other groups of staff?

She decided that she would bring these issues up at her next meeting with the unit general manager to seek some guidance from him regarding the overall philosophy on quality assurance in the district. The impression she gained from the quality assurance officer was that quality matters were being pushed down to unit level and, while this concurred very much with her management philosophy, she needed to understand how localised developments were integrated with the central initiatives taken by the district team.

She also wanted to explore the relationship between the more formal audit techniques and the problem-solving approach to criteria formulation and standard setting. When she had been director of nursing services in her previous job she had devised what she called a checklist for good practice. This document had contained over 100 statements on the care of the elderly service including items relating to the environment, provision of services, nursing records and information provided to patients.

She was not sure whether the use of such a checklist once a year would maintain the quality of the service to an acceptable level or whether the problem-solving approach she had been introduced to was more effective in the long run. Perhaps it was not a matter of which was better; rather, as she was beginning to discover, the question was which was the most appropriate method to use in a particular situation. As a manager she wanted to be given a selection of tools to use and be advised how to use them. And the design requirement as far as she was concerned was that they had to be simple, relevant, easy to use and work!

7.6   Summary

The manager plays an integral part in assuring the quality of the service. His/her role, however, is not to set standards; rather it is to facilitate the setting and achieving of agreed standards at the level of service delivery. In this respect the manager acts as a resource person, enabling and encouraging expert groups to get together to discuss their work in the light of successful interventions and those which have not been successful. Such communication can be encouraged to take part on a uni-or multidisciplinary level.

A second requirement is to ensure that when groups get together they have a working knowledge of criteria formulation, standard setting, and evaluation techniques. Thus, before a unit undertakes a quality assurance exercise it is the manager's responsibility to provide adequate introductory information, preparation and training for staff who will be expected to evaluate their practice. When this happens, either through formal workshops or by using trained facilitators at local level, the possibilities for quality improvement are quite significant.

Bibliography

A. Donabedian 'Some basic issues in evaluating the quality of health care', Issues in Evaluation Research, American Nurses' Association Invitational Conference, Kansas, pp. 3–28 (New York: ANA, 1975).

T. Douglas, *Basic Group Work*. (London: Tavistock Publications, 1978).

L. Fitzgerald and J. Murphy, *Installing Quality Circles: A Strategic Approach* (San Diego: University Associates Inc, 1982).

N. M. Formella and P. S. Schroeder, 'The Unit-Based System', *Nursing Quality Assurance. A Unit Based Approach*, Schroeder & Maibusch (eds) (Aspen Publication, 1984).

G. Harvey, 'Compiling a Directory', *Nursing Times*, **83**, No. 18 (1987) pp. 49–50.

H. Kendall and A. L. Kitson, 'Setting Standards', *Nursing Times*, **82**, No. 35 (1986) pp. 29–31.

A. L. Kitson, *A Framework for Quality – A Patient Centred Approach* (London: RCN, 1989).

A. L. Kitson and G. Harvey, *Nursing Quality Assurance Directory*, (London: RCN, 1987).

M. G. Mayer, R. B. Norby and A. B. Watson, *Quality Assurance Methods for Patient Care: Nursing Perspectives*, (New York: Appleton–Century-Crofts, 1977).

R. W. Napier and M. K. Gershenfeld, *Groups Theory and Experience*, 3rd ed. (Boston: Houghton Mifflin, 1982).

A. Pearson, *Nursing Quality Measurement. Quality Assurance Methods for Peer Review* (Chichester: Wiley 1987).

T. J. Peters and R. H. Waterman, *In Search of Excellence*, 2nd edn (New York: Harper and Row, 1986).

K. Robson, *The Journey to Excellence* (New York: Wiley, 1986).

L. D. Willis and M. C. Linwood, 'Measuring the Quality of Care', *Recent Advances in Nursing*. (Edinburgh: Churchill Livingstone, 1984).

D. Wright, 'An introduction to the evaluation of nursing care: a review of the literature. *Journal of Advanced Nursing*, **9**, No. 5 (1984) pp. 457–68.

Useful contact addresses

King's Fund Centre Quality Assurance Project
King's Fund Centre for Health Services Development'
126 Albert Street
London NW11
Tel: 01–267 6111

National Association of Quality Assurance (in Health Care)
Mamhilad House
Mamhilad Park Estate
Pontypool
Gwent NP4 OYP
Tel: 0495–762401

The British Quality Association (Health Services Sector Committee)
10 Grosvenor Gardens
London SW1 0DQ
Tel: 01–730 7154

Standards of Care Project
Royal College of Nursing
20 Cavendish Square   and
London W1M OAB
Tel: 01–409 3333

RCN Standards of Care Project
Institute of Nursing
Radcliffe Infirmary
Oxford
Tel: 0865 249891

8

Disciplinary Action and Organisational Consequences

Trevor Ride

8.1 Introduction

The theme of this chapter is the control and regulation of employees. This in itself is not limited to reprimanding deviant behaviour but can be considered in the arena of standards and quality assurance, as well as in the traditional personnel setting. These principles are not unique to nursing, or indeed health care, but can be applied to any organisational setting where the management of people is necessary.

8.1.1 Regulation of professionals

Professionals are answerable to a variety of people:

- Employers
- Patients
- Peers
- Public

If an incident occurs, the manager must ask:

- Is it a straightforward employment issue?
- Does it involve patients or clients?
- Is it a matter of professional conduct or, indeed, did the employee really do something wrong and is this ultimately a litigation issue?

118

Formal disciplinary action should be a last resort.

The ordinary 'telling somebody off' for something that happened in the normal course of employment should be quite acceptable and permissible within working relationships, and should not be exaggerated into full and formal disciplinary action on every occasion.

As professionals accept accountability given to them by virtue both of their training and of the formal responsibilities laid down by statutory bodies, then management must adjust its philosophy concerning the manner in which it imposes control and regulation. In a world which is becoming increasingly litigation conscious, formal procedures and a trigger-happy approach to disciplinary action can be seen in terms of people in general, and managers in particular, trying to 'cover their backs'. In practice, the rigid application of policies and procedures with disciplinary action hovering above can only serve to stifle professional practice. The balance has to be recognised, therefore, between professional autonomy and regulation of the worker.

Mistakes happen in all walks of life and one must always allow for genuine error. Does the employer have the right to expect anything different of the employee?

Action can be taken by the manager only on issues or in areas where the manager has the competence and authority to take such action. For example, a nurse can be disciplined by her local manager as a result of a drug error/incident, citing misconduct. Professional misconduct can be judged only by the Professional Conduct Committee of the United Kingdom Central Council for Nursing, Midwifery and Health Visiting in the UK.

8.1.2 Contractual regulation

Employee regulation is not, however, solely about issues of professional practice but may well be about straightforward employment issues, such as lateness, absenteeism or theft, which could happen in any working environment.

The employee's contractual obligations are naturally relevant in questions about absenteeism or lateness. Any disciplinary action in relation to absenteeism or lateness should be based on the employee's contractual obligations. But before jumping in on an issue of timekeeping, the manager must ask the preliminary question, 'Why has this happened?' and proceed to act under the guiding principle of reasonableness.

● Is it reasonable for the manager to consider the issue unacceptable?
● Is it reasonable for the manager to act in such a way over the issue?
● Is it reasonable for the employing authority to be committed to such action?

In most disciplinary procedures, there is ultimately some form of appeal to the employing authority. At this level, both the appellant and the local manager will be judged in terms of the reasonableness of the action. Situations can arise in which employing authorities do not uphold the action taken by the local manager, often to the consternation of the manager concerned. The question which has to be asked is, 'Was it reasonable for the manager to act in such a way?'

The subject of criminal charges and criminal convictions is also to be considered in the employment context of health care professionals in particular. A criminal charge in relation to the work of an employee, for example theft from work, misappropriation of drugs or assaulting a patient, are examples of such offences. Following an investigation, police may prefer charges. Even though the police may be investigating an incident, this does not mean that management need not instigate its own investigation which could lead to disciplinary action in terms of considering the suitability of the employee to remain in the employment. It is likely that the local investigation and disciplinary hearing by the employer would be speedier than that being made by the police and, indeed, delays in cases coming before the courts are not uncommon.

It is technically possible for an employee's disciplinary hearing to find a case not proven and for the subsequent court case to find the employee guilty. On the basis of conviction, it would not then be unreasonable for the employer to reconsider the case and take whatever disciplinary action seems appropriate, including if necessary the termination of employment.

The use by the employer of disciplinary action is of relevance in health care even to incidents occurring outside his or her employment. The use of disciplinary action, for example, on incidents that occur in hospital residences and involving off duty staff is inappropriate. The remedy if needed should be considered from the position of a landlord and not an employer. However, a criminal conviction which is unrelated to work could be grounds for action. Based on industrial tribunals case law, it has been upheld that, in the case of professionals, the employer has the right to expect a certain code of conduct outside the employment setting. A conviction for theft outside work has been upheld as grounds for terminating employment on the basis that it was reasonable for the employer not to expect such behaviour from a professional person.

There can be no hard and fast rules in these situations, the central issues are:

- What is reasonable?
- Are there mitigating circumstances?
- Does it affect performance in the job?

8.2 The case study

An experienced night sister was in charge of a large general hospital as well as being responsible for the cover of a paediatric unit staffed with trained nurses as well as students.

A 7-year-old boy was in severe abdominal pain on one of the paediatric wards following an appendectomy three days before, and the night sister was anxious that the child should be seen by a doctor as soon as possible. The senior surgical house officer was busy administering intravenous drugs on a surgical ward and told the night sister that he would come to see the child if she would take over administering the drugs for him. The night sister agreed to this and only one drug, cimetidine, remained to be given. This caused no particular problems for the sister as she was familiar with its administration and had given it many times at her last hospital.

The night sister thought nothing more of the events of that night. She was required to administer intravenous drugs as part of her duties, and, while the hospital's formal protocol included only a range of antibiotics and steroids for administration by approved nurses, she was familiar with cimetidine through previous experience. The patient on the surgical ward had received his drug and the child on the paediatric ward had been seen by the doctor.

Some days later, the sister on the surgical ward mentioned in passing to the nurse manager that the night sister had administered cimetidine which was not in accord with the normal procedure but that this had enabled the doctor to see another patient. There was no deliberate malicious intent on the part of the day sister in reporting the matter in this way, but the consequences soon became formalised.

Without any further warning, the night sister received what amounted to a standard letter asking her to attend an investigatory interview as a result of this incident, advising her that she might be accompanied by a friend or trade union representative and that disciplinary action might follow.

The interview took place in a formal setting and was conducted by the nurse manager in the presence of a personnel officer. The facts of the incident were not denied by the night sister and were proven. No mitigation was accepted and the outcome was that the night sister was formally warned not to breach the health authority's policies in such a manner again, otherwise this would lead to further disciplinary action which could result in dismissal. Furthermore, this warning was to remain on the night sister's personal record for a period of 12 months, after which it would be reviewed.

8.3   What are the problems?

● Is it a 'storm in a teacup'?
● Did the night sister contravene 'safe practice'?
● Did the manager have any alternative courses of action?

In analysing this incident, it should be noted that the nurse, as a professional, is answerable to a number of different people.

As far as the patient was concerned, he had been given a drug by a nurse rather than by a doctor. The correct drug had been administered in the prescribed format, at the correct time, with no adverse effects. As the nurse was familiar with the drug and its mode of administration, based on previous experience (albeit with another health authority), there was no question of the patient being put at any risk.

For the night sister, a duty of care existed in terms of the child with abdominal pain for whom she was primarily responsible and professionally accountable. The 'duty of care' is a legal term from which are then derived the tests of negligence. People have a duty to care – at its basic level this is to take reasonable care in whatever one is doing. The duty to care is also about ensuring that nothing harmful happens. 'Reasonable' care implies that another professional, with the same knowledge and ability, faced with the same situation, would act in a similar manner.

The night sister's action was the result of her analysis of the priorities, within the limits of manpower and skills available, for both her and the senior house officer. She also accepted a delegated task from the doctor. It could be argued that the doctor had no authority to delegate such a task to the night sister and had no way of knowing her competence to accept such a delegated task.

Within the partnerships that need to exist in the health care team, such delegations are, in practice, part of the partnership in trust that needs to exist between the various members of the team. Furthermore, experience shows that most nurses and doctors will work in such a way, particularly when priorities in patient care are the determining factors.

The night sister did not act outside the limits of her knowledge or abilities, having been trained in the use of such a drug in her previous employment. But she was answerable not only to the patient, but also to her employers, and what she did was to undertake a task contrary to the laid down policies of her employer. Furthermore, not only was she in breach of a policy, but she also did not appear to have any regard for the existence of such a policy when agreeing to undertake the task.

The other employee involved was, of course, the doctor. It was at the doctor's request that the night sister undertook to give the intravenous injection, and there was a presumption on the part of the doctor that she was competent to do so. His decision was also based on an issue of patient wellbeing and his ordering of the priorities. The fact that the action of the doctor in delegating the task is not called into question, either formally or informally, is of relevance itself in considering the reasonableness of the issue. This does not mean to say that every time a doctor delegates a task to a nurse and the nurse accepts it, that it occurs on the same basis. In addition, in this instance, neither of the parties was aware of the vicarious liability of their employer for all of their acts or omissions. Certainly the doctor did not appear to have any reservations in delegating the task to the nurse, who in turn only secured the patient's wellbeing.

A brief explanation of vicarious liability may help in understanding the situation. This, again, is a legal term derived from the master and servant principle in common law. The master is wholly responsible for the actions of his servant and can be held liable for them at law.

From the perspectives of the patient, the doctor and the nurse, it may be easy to conclude that the person who was wrong in her actions was, in fact, the nurse manager. Before reaching this conclusion, it is important to ask why she followed such a course of action. The matter was reported by the day sister, and at that point the nurse manager became aware of a breach of the policies laid down on behalf of the employer, namely the health authority.

The fact that nothing untoward happened to the patient is immaterial in this respect, in that any employer is able to lay down terms and conditions of employment or, in this case, rules to be followed by employees. Rules regarding the conduct of clinical practice may vary from employer to employer but, in each instance, it can usually be demonstrated that they have been made for some good reason, at least locally. In this instance, the rules relate to those members of staff permitted to give intravenous drugs. It was as an officer upholding these rules, that the nurse manager acted. It can therefore be considered that such rules were necessary in that particular hospital, as indeed are many rules governing both employment and professional practice in many organisations.

It could also be argued that if the nurse manager had not acted, then negligence could be implied on her part since clearly such rules are formulated to protect the business of the employer. Under the master and servant principles of common law, should anything have gone wrong as a result of the nurse administering the injection, then the patient could have taken litigation for negligence, not only against the night sister, but also against the employing authority through vicarious liability. The defence, therefore, on behalf of the employer, would be that the employee was in breach of the employer's own rules regarding the incident.

8.4   Did the manager have any alternative courses of action?

In addition to the legal aspect of this case, consideration should also be given to the nature of the events. Over and above establishing that the night sister did something wrong, although the patient was not put at risk, the next issue is to analyse how the investigation was handled and discipline conducted. The investigation led straight into formal action involving the initial letter summoning the sister to the meeting.

Why did the manager, in wanting to find out what occurred, move so quickly into a formal procedure? The individual circumstances of each case need to be taken into account, but the fact that formal procedures may exist for a manager to use does not mean necessarily that they need be used in every instance.

Consideration should always be given to an informal discussion and investigation if it is believed that this will not be prejudicial to the final outcome, or indeed, if the nature of the incident can clearly justify such action. It may well have been, in this instance, that an informal discussion between the night sister and nurse manager would have indicated the following:

● Particular medical staffing problems at night
● Issues of medical and nursing workload
● The extent to which the administration of intravenous drugs affects the workload of night sisters
● The appropriateness of the particular policies and practices in this hospital and a range of other possible issues

All of these could have been considered to have been a reasonable management response forming a review of practices after the incident. As happened in this case, a formal 'quasi-judicial' hearing took place, where, in essence the night sister was found guilty and was 'sentenced' to have a formal record of her breach of her employer's policies made on her personal file. The length of time that this warning would remain in force and the implied consequences of any further breach appear to be the natural progression once the disciplinary process was started.

Questions can be asked as to why, on an issue of clinical practice, the disciplinary sanction is that of a time constraint for not repeating the offence and why the warning would only remain on file for a year pending review. This again reflects the inappropriateness of such formalities on an issue that could be considered to be clinical malpractice.

Essentially, the written warning serves only as a formal record for all parties concerned, stating what has happened and what, if any, sanctions have been applied. The purpose would be better served if the record was about setting performance targets, identifying and providing for training needs and performance review. If, for professional reasons, it is wrong for something to happen, then it is always wrong and not just for a specified period of time!

8.5   Winners or losers?

There have been no winners or losers in this incident.

● The night sister has been disciplined for doing what she thought was best for her patient. Perhaps in other settings she would have been supported for ensuring patient safety
● The importance of the doctor's contribution to the situation has been disregarded because in structural terms the nurse manager had no authority over the doctor. Future tensions may develop between nursing and medical staff
● The nurse manager has upheld the policies of the employing organisation but may well have lost credibility
● The patient received the appropriate care at the correct time from a person trained in this particular procedure

To all intents and purposes, the business of the hospital can continue.

What does not appear to have come out of this incident is any indication of the contribution that the incident and its investigation has made to the management and organisation of the hospital. This includes the issues of the administration of intravenous drugs at night and the use and conduct of the disciplinary procedure. It is appropriate then to look at these issues in terms of what can be done when things go wrong.

8.6 What are the general principles?

When something has happened or something has gone wrong, it is as important to ask the question 'Why has this happened?' as it is to establish what has happened. Look at what are the real consequences as opposed to what are the assumed consequences of the issue. The question – 'What has happened' – always seems to make the assumption that something has actually gone wrong and some party has been 'injured'. This, as in the case study, need not be so. If, for whatever reasons, actions have been taken which lie outside procedures, the problem then becomes more a management matter in terms of organisational systems. This leads to the question 'Why has this happened?'

It is sometimes easy in the heat of the moment, in issues of professional or employee conduct, to jump hastily to conclusions. Much can be gained from standing back and putting yourself into the situation. Is the conduct at work of a professional fundamentally a professional issue requiring a professional perspective? Is it a matter of clinical practice? In incidents such as the administration of drugs, look at what is the normal practice in the everyday course of events on a ward. It may well be that what is discovered to be inappropriate in the view of management has, in fact, been custom and practice in the hospital for some time. This does not imply that either side is right or wrong, but that the way in which an issue is handled should be influenced by the principle of reasonable conduct.

Supposing, for example, nurses are caught drinking tea on the ward. It is easy to say that this is the theft of hospital property, but to what extent are alternative facilities being provided? Is the organisation actually benefiting from nurses staying on the ward adjacent to patient areas? There are a whole range of grey issues that need to be considered by looking at the fairness or reasonableness of decisions and conduct.

Such an incident is quite different from the night nurse who is found asleep on duty. Again, it should be asked why this has happened, but the consequences of what has happened are singularly different. Once again, the principle of what is reasonable to expect must apply.

The standard of conduct or performance which can be expected is that which it is reasonable to expect from anyone in the same position with the same experience, knowledge and responsibility. In order to determine this, it is sometimes necessary for managers in the course of the investigation to put themselves in the position of the employee, so that they can reflect on the circumstances that might apply.

Ultimately, managers must make decisions based either on evidence, demonstrable probability or the corporate conduct and performance that, based on their own experience and judgements, they know should be expected in such a setting. This is part of the risk of management, and may eventually rest upon a single judgement on the part of the manager as to what is or is not acceptable.

Bibliography

Code of Practice (London: ACAS 1980).
Code of Professional Conduct for the Nurse, the Midwife and the Health Visitor (London: UKCC, 1984).
Employment Act 1980 (London: HMSO, 1980).
Employment Act 1982 (London: HMSO, 1982).
Employment Protection Act 1975 (London: HMSO, 1975).
Employment Protection (Consolidation) Act 1978 (London: HMSO, 1978).
C. Hancock, 'Giving Advice at Work', *Health Services Manpower Review* (University of Keele, 1983).
Nurses Rules: Statutory Instruments (London: HMSO).
R. Pyne, *Professional Discipline in Nursing* (Oxford: Blackwell, 1981).
RCN Stewards Handbook (London: RCN, 1982).
The Administration of Medicines (London: UKCC, 1985).
The Extending Role of the Clinical Nurse. Legal Implications and Training Requirements, (HC(77)22) (London: DHSS, 1977).

9
Staffing Matters
Tom Keighley

9.1 Introduction

The history of health care in the United Kingdom is one that reflects the availability of two major resources: money to pay for the provision of the service and people to deliver it. Permanent solutions to the difficulty of ensuring the availability of both have not been found.

Events such as the two world wars have forced change on the professions by causing the government to impose central controls, particularly on the availability of manpower. The cyclical nature of the demographic roller-coaster has resulted in three 'baby-booms' in the past 70 years, which have, at least temporarily, helped to relieve pressure on workforce shortage. However, for the first time since the great depression of the 1850s, the population of the UK has fallen below replacement level and is continuing to fall. This means that managers in the health service face a challenge of unparalleled proportions.

In considering a response to this challenge, four areas are critical and, indeed, always have been:

- Staffing requirements
- Recruitment
- Retention
- Utilisation

Two other issues have a higher priority than used to be the case in the past:

- Succession planning
- Equal opportunities

These can often appear to contradict each other. They need to be managed effectively if there is to be some real equality in the processes of appointment, as well as being able to use vacancies to ensure that individual potential is developed and the next generation of senior staff is produced. Finally, there is a need to consider the longer term future of health care staffing in both professional and political terms.

9.2 Case study – opening a 5-day ward

Improvements, particularly in anaesthetics and, to a lesser extent in surgical technique and analgesia, have resulted in a diminishing number of people requiring hospital admission for a period of time longer than 5 days and 4 nights. Many health authorities have been developing 5-day units as a way of maximising the use of resources.

Such exercises challenge managers to determine the nature of the health service they require; to meet the needs of the population they serve; to identify the human resources available to provide services to meet the needs of the community; to develop staff in such a way as to be able to meet those needs and finally to evaluate the effect of the service being provided.

While the opening of a 5-day ward may appear to be a comparatively minor development, it represents a fundamental change in the traditional nature of the service and suggests that new principles of service delivery apply.

In planning a 5-day ward, the traditional view of staffing needs to be abandoned. First, the provision is for four 24-hour periods and usually one complete day shift, because a 5-day ward runs for only 4 nights. Second, the intensity of the care tends to peak early in the week, Monday lunchtime to Wednesday afternoon, before tailing off towards Friday. Third, there is a need for good communication with relatives and GPs as patient throughput is likely to be high, so the balance of staff may have a higher number of ward clerks than average for the rest of the unit.

As all staff are a finite resource, the balance achieved will depend on availability. This is more likely to depend on a local population as the shifts can be more rigid but with a greater emphasis on qualified staff, particularly when the patient dependency is highest. Also, as 5-day wards tend to replace 7-day wards, staff should be available from within the organisation but re-orientation and some development may be required.

9.3 Problems and solutions

9.3.1 Staffing requirements

It is comparatively rare within the National Health Service to be able to create a service from new. So often, development is a process of incrementalism, as one new activity is added to another, usually as a result of competition between numerous groups of health care professionals, and on the basis of the extended negotiations needed to meet the demands of those same professionals. The development of a 5-day ward gives the opportunity to look at the principles which govern the provision of service in a way which incremental developments do not.

In determining service provision, two processes need to be considered (Figure 9.1).

Figure 9.1 Determining service

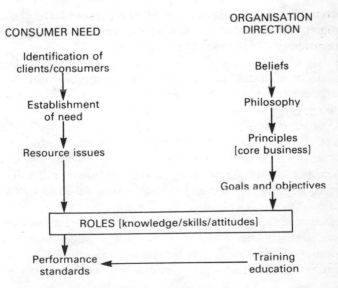

Figure 9.1 draws together consumer need and organisational direction. Central to service provision is the clarification of the roles of individuals. The righthand side of the figure indicates the steps an organisation may take if it wishes to identify the roles to be created for the achievement of its goals and objectives. The lefthand side of the diagram describes the process of community diagnosis which can equally validly lead to the identification of appropriate professional roles. Sadly, the two processes are rarely done in conjunction. If attempted, feedback into both processes will ideally occur as the role definitions emerge. Once the roles have been agreed, performance standards should be determined. Training and education should relate to producing individuals to work to the performance standard of the role definition.

A 5-day ward should emerge from a process such as this. Consumers in a health service have needs which are best met with the minimum period in hospital. Similarly, health authorities want patients in hospital for as short a period as possible. Happily, the advances in technology and in caring techniques have improved as health care professionals have developed their roles. This means that with improved performance, new standards can be set. In this scenario, a 5-day ward becomes the accepted standard of service provision for all parties concerned.

The staff of the National Health Service, because of the bias to training within hospitals, may see care given within such institutions as being better in some sense than that which is delivered within the community. To provide a sound staff base for a development such as a 5-day ward, it is essential to produce individuals who perceive the delivery of care in a much more eclectic manner. This does not apply only to nurses, but nursing has been a profession in which the work within a hospital has taken primacy over the work within the community. In order to be able to introduce a 5-day ward, it is essential to understand the philosophies and values which will influence and affect the staff who may have to change both their practice and their roles.

In creating such developments, the initial point of discussion is so often the funding of the service. Classically, this is the wrong place to start. Any debate which asks how much can one get for the money available, rather than having initially decided the nature of the service and the principles that will be used to determine the delivery of that service, is having a debate about the means rather than the ends.

People are the major resource within the health service and therefore discussions should start with a clear view of the nature of the service to be provided and the roles that will be required to be fulfilled if that service is to exist. The roles can be adjusted, redefined and revised until an appropriate combination of skills is agreed. Such agreement can then be put alongside the physical environment in which care will be delivered and ultimately discussions can take place about the cost and the various staffing permutations available.

Increasingly, managers have to consider the alternatives to such complex discussions within the NHS as they are time consuming and not always productive. One alternative is to stick with the current provision of service. Another is to explore what is available within the private sector. Finally, though not yet in this country, there is the possibility of voluntary sector involvement.

There are wide-ranging alternatives available to a manager who is confronted with the need either to rationalise the use of resources or to develop a more effective way of providing a service. Exploring and evaluating them in a rational manner is time consuming, but the alternative is to be rushed into a service which, while appearing to be more effective, cannot be staffed and will, therefore, not provide the type or kind of service which was anticipated.

One area well worth exploring is the skill base of staff. The term skill base refers to that range of abilities and competencies with which an individual is endowed on completing some form of training. If, therefore, a registered nurse is appointed in contrast to an enrolled nurse, the manager should expect a significant difference in the range of abilities that the individual employee brings to the task in hand.

Being clear about skill bases has not been one of the major qualities of nurse managers in the past. When asked why a registered nurse is being appointed in preference to an enrolled nurse, the answer is often in the realm of availability and professional judgement rather than the more pragmatic and, perhaps, rational response which rests on a clear understanding of the abilities which that individual may have to bring to the post.

The manager has choices to make. These may partly be forced by the availability of staff but, initially, some thought must be given to the different varieties of combinations available in principle, and, indeed, the degree of flexibility that will be required in order to provide a service. The traditional division of 40 per cent qualified to 30 per cent unqualified means that managers are prepared to work with a staffing level that is made up of 60 per cent unqualified staff and, therefore, staff who cannot take direct responsibility for the work they are undertaking.

There is a temptation with a 5-day ward to believe that such an arrangement is acceptable as the care being delivered may appear to be comparatively minor. An alternative view is to see the service in a 5-day ward as being in the forefront of care provision. The improvements in technology and procedures mean that an increasing range of types of care can be delivered, demanding an increasing level of ability among the nursing staff, where there is a quick turnover of patients, an intensity of care and a very real opportunity for errors caused by time pressures.

The decision might, therefore, be to exclude learners from such an area or, indeed, to exclude untrained staff and run the unit with either a fully qualified complement of staff or combined with staff in training. Such decisions will be based on the type and volume of surgical patients going through that unit and the level of expertise required from the staff working there. One possibility might be to employ staff who work both within the unit and in the community when the patients are discharged. Such a rotational system offers some district nurses the opportunity to work in a ward environment while appropriately trained ward staff will be able to follow up cases directly into the community.

Much will depend on whether these are patients who cannot be treated in a day ward but who require an overnight stay, or whether they are patients who traditionally might have required at least 7 days in a ward and are now being treated in a span of 5 days and 4 nights with enhanced community care on discharge.

The level of patient or client dependency needs to be agreed as part of the definition of professional roles and operational policies. What must be challenged are the traditions instilled in staff by years of previous practice and training. There may, of course, be a need for updating, and the provision of postbasic courses on a regular basis should be a feature of all areas in which care is delivered. This is especially so in areas where there is a rapid throughput of patients and rapid change in the techniques of care delivery.

9.3.2   Recruitment

Recruitment should not be considered in isolation from retention and utilisation. Retaining staff and utilising them more effectively and efficiently will affect recruitment activity significantly. There is always the assumption in any recruitment initiative that the planned service needs have been identified and a clear idea of the number and type of staff required to meet those service needs has been formulated. [This should be the case in a new unit.]

The two major recruitment attractions are pay and terms and conditions of employment. The nursing clinical grading review has loosened up the pay situation, but terms and conditions remain standard and are used too often as a negotiable maximum rather than an obligatory minimum. Recruitment can best be considered under five headings:

● Supply
● Information
● Image and publicity
● Pay
● Working conditions

The supply of professional staff is often dependent on the provision of training at both basic and postbasic levels. For example, back-to-nursing courses that are sufficiently flexible to attract people from all nursing disciplines are a useful adjunct to this, as are access courses for those in the pre-nursing age groups and for mature starters. Currently very popular is the use of overseas recruitment, particularly Southern Ireland. Less popular, but in the longer term a more secure source of recruits, is the development of Youth Training Schemes (YTS) in the NHS. Sources of development and preparation for recruitment should include a full range of distance learning options from

Business and Technical Education Colleges [BTec] to the Open University. There is also a need to plan for the recruitment of support staff, in particular porters, catering staff and administrative and clerical staff.

The information aspect of recruitment falls into two parts. First, there is the need to analyse the labour market to identify recruitment potential. This includes learning about local competition, transport networks, catchment areas and the local costs of facilities such as housing and leisure. The second part of recruitment information is to be knowledgeable about the current workforce. This includes knowing percentages of staff working part-time and by gender, grade, occupational group, location and age. This enables the two types of information to be correlated and recruitment efforts focussed.

In recruitment, image and publicity are crucial. Immediately recognisable logos or letter patterns lead to recognition and identification with the organisation. The development of advertising materials, large postal drops [100000 +], links with local groups, car stickers, open days, coffee mornings/cheese and wine evenings, appointment of recruitment officers and use of job centres all develop a higher local profile. National profiles can be improved by use of more imaginative journals for advertising, particularly ethnic newspapers, school-age publications and involvement in national initiatives and conferences. The local image can be enhanced by developing unique uniforms for staff and having a local reputation as a 'good employer'. Good personnel practices are an essential element of this.

Pay and recruitment is currently an uncertain area with the impact of clinical grading reviews still to be worked through. However, some elements can be used to increase the value of pay received. This includes the development of car leasing schemes, of joint mortgage and loan schemes, as well as the promotion of the use of the NHS mortgage scheme. On a longer timescale, there is the possibility of exploring pay scales for improvements in pay, adopting a flexible attitude to choice of starting incremental point, and of lobbying for longer incremental scales.

Finally, there is much that can be done to influence working conditions. Flexible work patterns, especially if introduced as an initiative by senior staff, can help a new unit meet its own problems. Flexitime working and job-sharing can follow. The use of nursing banks enables more flexible shift patterns to develop. The establishment of a nurse-returners bureau, a reservist scheme (a system which tracks nurses in an authority with annual checks on availability), and a policy on career breaks maximises the use of nurses in the local population.

More obvious approaches include crèches, health authority child minders, holiday clubs, on-site shopping facilities and supportive counselling for working parents. Security for night staff in particular, transport clubs for those working irregular hours, a mentoring system for all new joiners and good 'starter' packs all influence recruitment and begin to build the process of retention.

9.3.3 Retention

The art of keeping staff is to be aware of the reasons for leaving.

The approach shown in Figure 9.2 permits managers to identify areas of particular concern, to focus investigation and to set up monitoring systems. Methods for investigating turnover can be *post hoc* or barametric.

Figure 9.2 Identification of problem areas

Basic information		Type of leaver
Length of service		Voluntary
Age	Needs to be	Involuntary
Gender	analysed under	Retirement
Grade	the headings of	Maternity reasons
Department		Dismissal

Exit interviews and separation questionnaires are two typical *post hoc* methods, subject to 'post-hoc rationalisation' and, therefore, to be used with care. Barametric methods are those processes of analysis which monitor known staffing problems and identify new difficulties. Staff satisfaction surveys and sample interviewing by senior staff of junior staff are typical and effective methods. Areas worth particular consideration in any study of staff retention include:

● Pay
● Management style
● Nature of the work
● Working conditions

Reference has already been made to the difficulty encountered in manipulating pay. However, service bonuses, long service
awards, performance related pay used in tandem with an
individual performance review system and the payment of
overtime rather than time off in lieu can all have a positive effect
on retention.

Perhaps less tangible, but no less important, is management
style. There is clearly a need to enhance the interpersonal skills
of managers and to develop the communication networks and
consultative machinery. The development of exemplary styles
of leadership encourages self-reliance and risk taking. If this is
done within a framework that has agreed and meaningful
philosophies, as well as a supportive administration, which
encourages innovation and experimentation, a sense of purpose
and direction will emerge.

Examining the nature of the work undertaken by staff gives
useful insight into the issue of retention. People remain where
they experience high levels of self-fulfilment. This requires
managers to determine and establish appropriate skill mixes,
staff–patient ratios, and to use labour substitution where necessary. The use of staff attitude surveys, the improvement of
development opportunities and the formalisation of career planning give staff a sense of belonging. A counselling service can
both help to deal with difficulties arising during employment as
well as preventing people from making the wrong career moves.
The counselling service should provide training for managers
to recognise stress in staff and the manager's role in alleviating
it.

Some mention has already been made about the effect of
working conditions on recruitment. They also affect retention.
Further measures worth considering include:

● Reducing weekend working and minimising staff rotation.
● Use of job swaps
● The development of career-break policies

If possible, a pleasant working atmosphere should be created on the ward with good staff social facilities, peer-group support, in-house newsletters and incentive/bonus schemes for good health records or outstanding through-put achievements. The work of managers can be focused on:

- Efforts to regulate and control workload
- Use of occupational health facilities to control absence
- Dealing rapidly with individual grading reviews
- The acquisition of good personnel skills by all managers

This combination of factors will begin to make people believe they are wanted in an organisation and appreciated for what they do.

Loyalty is a term which is rarely heard within the NHS but has something to do with the degree of involvement or ownership that staff have about the organisation in which they work. Sadly, public statements by politicians, professional organisations and, on occasions, senior managers within the health service, have often led staff to believe that they are an unimportant and dispensable part of an organisation.

To overcome this, it is necessary to enable change to occur through the staff themselves and to facilitate the development of change from the grassroots. A number of techniques are available for undertaking this.

One that works particularly well when bringing in new initiatives is the development of a number of quality circles. Such groups not only produce a far richer range of solutions to problems but ensure that individuals who will be working within the service feel they have a contribution to make. They develop their service in a way which reflects both their significant expertise and ability as well as the realisation that it is first-line staff, those who have the closest contact with the recipients of the service, who know best how to deliver that service.

9.3.4 Utilisation

Methods to improve the utilisation of staff on the ward can be both mechanistic and behavioural. Both approaches require target establishments to be identified, skill mixes agreed and workloads determined. In the future, there will be increasing pressure to match workload to staff as available workers become an increasingly rare commodity. Mechanistic methods match workforce to workload. Behavioural approaches attempt to engender organisational identification and personal commitment to it by staff.

Workload measurement and staff deployment starts with community diagnosis as described earlier, undertaken in parallel with health authority-wide workforce planning exercises. Annual planning cycles facilitate this. At a local level, managers need to review skill mix and develop occasional mechanisms to augment baseline staffing in a crisis. There is a need for contingency planning and to review how changes in medical practice affect staff utilisation. Similarly, the building and maintenance programme for the ward will affect staff utilisation and needs to be well planned and coordinated to maximise staff availability.

9.3.5   Succession planning

Currently a very popular notion, succession planning is not something that has been well thought through. It is based on the idea that the current generation of workers has a responsibility to ensure the development of the next generation. Clearly, some individuals are recognised as being more able than others. The nature of that enhanced ability is often unclear. Succession planning ensures that these individuals experience the types of development which will best equip them to develop leadership potential and thus to acquire senior posts.

A 5-day ward is a good environment for the development of leadership potential. The range of demands on individuals, and the need to work within constraints, will mark out people of ability, energy and creativity. Their development may be through professional or managerial courses or through study for higher degrees. It is often difficult to know what is the best form of systematic development. Good succession planning tailors the development to the abilities and needs of individuals. Potential leaders should then be encouraged to apply for the challenging posts which they themselves are perhaps still uncertain about their ability to fulfil. A large part of succession planning is enabling people to be stretched, but always with the intention of producing the next generation of key people.

Succession planning has not been well thought through in many organisations because it runs counter to two major factors currently operating in the NHS. The first is that to plan successors to current post-holders suggests that those posts will continue in some form. While it is true that senior posts are likely to remain in whatever structure the health service takes, and that individuals need to be prepared to take them, the impact of previous reorganisations in 1974, 1982 and 1984 suggest that longer term activities such as succession planning can be disrupted for very long periods. The second antipathetic factor affecting succession planning is the adoption of equal opportunity policies.

9.3.6 *Equal opportunities*

Many health authorities have formulated equal opportunity policies. Sadly, very few have made them a reality of organisational life. When starting from scratch, as with a new unit, the need for such a policy is essential as a guide to the processes of appointment and, indeed, promotion. Such a policy should cover all aspects of recruitment, retention and staff utilisation.

From the moment advertising for posts is considered, the process should be clear to everyone. It should have the agreement of management and staff. Such policies should require formal job descriptions to be agreed for all posts. Person specifications should also be drawn up at the same time as the job description, not when the shortlisted candidates are sitting in the anteroom waiting to be interviewed. All enquirers and applicants for posts should be dealt with in a sensitive but standard manner which encourages applications, but prevents discrimination.

When shortlisting, the criteria should be job related and not require any unnecessary skill or qualification. Interviewing should never be done alone and the questions asked should relate directly to the post to be filled. A record of all interviews should be kept. When considering people for training, especially when they are already in post, it is permissible to exercise a degree of positive discrimination. Selection tests should not indirectly discriminate and all occupational qualifications should be genuine requirements. Clearly, there is a need for the policy to be monitored to ensure that it is applied to all cases.

9.4 Summary

The development of new services provides nurse managers with the opportunity to review the nature of the nursing contribution as well as to consider its historical practice. The need is to emphasise that which is good from the past and which has a role to play in the future as well as producing nurses who have a degree of flexibility which enables them to respond creatively to the challenges of the future.

The management of staffing and of all workforces within the health service in the future will depend on being able to induce that degree of creativity and flexibility which ensures that the service continuously adjusts and evolves to respond to the needs of the community it is trying to serve. The challenge for managers is to value their workforce in such a way which enables them to lead the change rather than having to have the change imposed.

Bibliography

S. Bevan, *The Management of Labour Turnover*, IMS Report No. 137 (London: IMS, 1984).

N. Bosanquet, and K. Gerard, *Nursing Manpower: Recent Trends and Policy Options*, Discussion Paper No. 9 (Centre for Health Economics, University of York, 1985).

D. Dean, *Manpower Solutions* (London: RCN/Scutari, 1987).

National audit office, *NHS: Control of Nursing Manpower*, Report of the Comptroller and Auditor General (London: HMSO, 1985).

The Women Returners Network, *Returning to Work – Education and Training for Women 1987* (London: Longman, 1987).

10
Managing Industrial Relations
Gordon Hemsley

10.1 Introduction

This chapter has the objective of encouraging readers to think how, as managers, they are going to encourage increased productivity in their workforce. It uses a case study to highlight a challenge a manager faced and demonstrates strategies that could have been taken and some obvious pitfalls to be avoided.

One of the major pressures in the health service is the constant search for cost improvement measures. Since on average 70 per cent of the total costs are staffing costs, a key area of continuing improvement will be the effective use of labour.

In the economy as a whole since 1979, the Conservative government has sought to improve productivity and make workers more aware of the economic consequences of their actions. In the latest data published by the Department of Employment, the progressive decline in the number of strikes has continued since a peak reached in 1979. However, the proportion of strikes caused by disputes over 'working practices' has increased to about 40 per cent of all strikes. This is most probably caused by management seeking to improve on productivity. Many of the large state-owned organisations such as British Steel, the National Coal Board and British Airways have made significant gains, as has much of the private sector. To some extent the health service has been protected from the blast of competition. Will it be so in the future?

In the case study the desire of a manager to improve overall productivity is the root cause of a dispute. She is forced to do something because of perceived low productivity.

has changed. Management style has also changed and the more successful managers are prepared to keep employees informed and to work to obtain commitment from their staff. In looking at the case study these points need to be borne in mind.

10.2   Case study

A new unit general manager (UGM) with a nursing background was appointed to a hospital in November 1985. This was her first general management post and she decided that during her first six months she needed to stand back and assess the performance of the unit in general, and her managers in particular. She was, however, determined through past experience as a nurse that the support services provided to nursing must be improved.

She quickly became very concerned over the performance of the works team; many jobs were not completed on time and they rarely met budget. She had noticed, in walking around the hospital, that often the men on jobs were not actually working. Her relationship with the unit works manager was not good and she found him evasive in his response to her concern. He also had health problems and resented working for a UGM rather than the district general manager (DGM).

The UGM decided, in the spring of 1986, that a change had to be made at the top of the organisation. This was discussed with the DGM and she arranged for the works manager to be transferred to district. She resolved that the new appointee would be both much more attuned to management and more dynamic, and that the appointment should come from outside the district to bring a fresh view. The post was advertised externally in June 1986.

In the interim period the deputy unit works manager who had worked his way up from the shop floor was asked to act in the position. After two readvertisements a successful candidate was found and took up post in February 1987. The deputy manager made it clear to colleagues that he much resented this outsider coming into a post which he had felt he had filled successfully for several months.

The unit works department was responsible for both maintenance of building and equipment and also new building work. The workforce covered a wide variety of trades and were represented by several trade unions. In the spring of 1987 two first line supervisors left, and the unit works manager relied on his deputy to appoint two new supervisors. He did not attend the interviews because he was away from the hospital on a course but was concerned on his return to be met by a small deputation protesting at the appointments. It was alleged that the interviews had not been fair and that the district equal opportunities policy had not been followed. He attempted to smooth over the problem and he felt he had succeeded.

Budgets continued to be overspent and the UGM pressed for improvement. The level of the complaints about delays also grew and the unit works manager therefore decided to concentrate his workforce on maintenance work only. He felt that putting new work out for tender would bring a more competitive edge, and also allow him to concentrate his own workforce on key maintenance. This, of course, meant that the earnings of his own workforce would drop because of the reduction in weekend and overtime working.

The unit works manager knew the productivity of his in-house force was low, and in conjunction with his deputy, decided to determine the causes. He arranged for a small team to carry out activity sampling and communicated this decision to the workforce through his deputy and the stewards. At the same time he instructed his supervisors to tighten up, particularly on areas such as sickness absence and poor time-keeping.

In January 1988 there was a violent argument between one of the new supervisors and one of his men, who had come from the West Indies as a child, which eventually ended with a punch being thrown at the supervisor. The argument was over time-keeping. The unit works manager decided that summary dismissal was the only way he could stamp the authority of management and accordingly summoned the alleged assailant to his office and dismissed him summarily.

Later that day the workforce held a meeting and decided to stop work immediately and set up a picket line demanding the reinstatment of the dismissed worker and the disciplining of the supervisor for a racist remark.

10.3 Problems and solutions

10.3.1 *What caused the dispute?*

The mining industry describes the type of dispute in the case study as a 'ragout' – a dispute where a series of events or conditions causes tempers to become short, culminating in an incident which finally brings the industrial relations problems to a head. Disputes are easy to cause, but can be complex to solve and invariably cause loss of face. Perhaps if all levels of management had behaved differently no dispute would have arisen.

All managers in the health service work to Whitley Council rules; all health authorities have grievance and dispute procedures; most, if not all, have equal opportunities policies and all should have rules on who has authority to dismiss. Managers also need to have a clear understanding of legislation in this field. Much has been made in recent years of legislation which limits the scope of unions and which requires, for example, ballots to be held before strikes or restricts the right of the union to take secondary action.

There is, however, also legislation which was introduced to restrict the right of employers to take unilateral action and, in the case study, potential claims could be made for unfair dismissal or for discrimination on grounds of race. Managers cannot be expected to know in detail all the legislation, but they do need a broad understanding and they do need to take proper professional advice from personnel staff.

The case study can be looked at from a number of different points of view and these are described below. A series of questions are posed about the actions and attitudes of various interested parties.

10.3.2 *District general manager*

He was responsible for the appointment of a nurse to a UGM position.

● What support and guidance did the DGM give to help the UGM settle into the job?

- Was the DGM aware of possible prejudice by the UGM concerning support services?
- Did the DGM need to influence events more as they developed? Should there, for example, have been a discussion with all UGMs and district works teams about efficiency?

10.3.3 Unit general manager

The person pressing for change is arguably the person ultimately responsible for the strike.

- Did she jump to conclusions over the efficiency of the works group?
- Where could she have obtained professional advice?
- Could she had handled her personal relationships with the old unit works manager differently?
- When she decided to make a new appointment did she talk to the second in command? Did she cause false expectations to arise?
- How did she communicate her concerns over efficiency to her staff?
- Could she have involved her personnel officer?
- How is she going to resolve the dispute?

10.3.4 Unit works manager

- Did he get appropriate guidance from his manager?
- Was he correct to delegate the responsibility for making key appointments to his disaffected deputy?
- Should he have stopped construction work unilaterally without discussion?
- How should he have communicated with staff?
- Did he introduce activity sampling correctly and how would he have used the results?
- Should he have smoothed over the questions of the appointment of the supervisors?
- Should he have dismissed the man who threw the punch?

10.3.5 Deputy unit works manager

- Did he clearly understand why his boss was moved and why he was not promoted?

● Did he support his new boss?
● *Did he discriminate at interview?*

Readers might like to think through similar questions over the role of stewards, first level supervision, union officials and unit personnel. More importantly, managers need to put themselves in the same position as the staff. How would you feel if you had a critical manager who had introduced work study, called in contractors, cut earnings, allowed discriminatory interviews, failed to communicate and unilaterally sacked a respected colleague?

10.4   Dispute resolution

The resolution of disputes is never easy, because individuals are forced into polarised positions. The whole theme of this chapter is that managers can achieve objectives and make changes without getting into strike situations. Two key factors need to be borne in mind when discussing strikes; they are contagious and reinfection is easy. Prevention is better than cure!

In this case study there are a number of ways of resolving the issue. In the situation described, union officials could strongly urge their members to return to work pending an investigation into the issue. The UGM could ask to review the dismissal and ask that the dismissed employee be suspended on full pay.

In this way immediate heat could be take out of the situation. If necessary the Independent Arbitration and Conciliation Service could be involved. If, for example, the man who was dismissed appealed to an industrial tribunal against dismissal or made a complaint alleging racial discrimination, ACAS would become involved before a tribunal heard the case. In 1987 ACAS conciliated in approximately 1500 disputes as well as providing an individual arbitration service. In fact, ACAS annually handles over 50000 individual cases and resolves about 70 per cent of these before a tribunal. One key resource to remember is that free advice is available from experienced staff working either for ACAS or for the Equal Opportunities Commission.

10.5   How could the objectives be achieved?

The new UGM, coming fresh into general management in 1985, needed to stand back and assess the situation. She also needed to make a major effort to understand her works department and the pressures on them. A new manager coming from a specialist background does need to understand the culture and working of her new department.

Unlike nursing or medicine, staff in works departments do not come from a purely NHS background. Frequently they have served apprenticeships elsewhere and are proud of their skills. Their trade unions are organised differently and their fulltime officials normally have responsibility for a wide range of industries. Their union branches are not NHS based but have members from a wide variety of sources.

The effectiveness of a workforce depends on good planning, organisation and supervision; an area where some fall down. The UGM needed to understand the planning process to ensure that adequate time and money was allowed. At times the workforce can be blamed when the fault lies elsewhere! In our private lives we are all used to optimistic quotes on delivery and cost. It also happens in the NHS.

Demarcation has become a much abused word and undoubtedly does affect productivity. On the other hand no manager would condone, for example, a painter fiddling with complex wiring, merely because the electrician had been delayed on another job. Similarly the co-ordination and delivery of materials might be causing delays. How aware was the UGM of potential delays caused by this type of problem?

In fact, because of the factors highlighted above, the individual craftsman is likely to spend less than half his working time in a productive manner. It seems surprising, but next time you have work done in your house, watch!

The UGM therefore needed to understand the working of her works department, the culture and the background to the problems. She made a major decision in deciding to replace her works manager. Clearly in all walks of life it is necessary to replace managers from time to time, but it does need to be handled in a sensible way. One of the areas the NHS has not been good at in the past is setting objectives and reviewing individual performance against them. It is too easy to remove a manager because of personal antipathy without measuring and seeking to improve his effectiveness. The removal of the manager in the case study may have caused all sorts of alarm bells to ring in the minds of the rest of the department.

The desire to bring in a manager from outside was a very clear signal that all was not well and that change was needed. When management changes are being made, these need to be planned and properly communicated. It is likely that latent hostility was established at this stage which eventually was one of the causes of the strike. Obviously the second in line did not understand the reasons why he did not get the job.

Staff care about management changes when they are affected, and the UGM could have prepared the ground. Quite clearly the second in line needed to be talked to and given a thorough explanation of his position. He might also be given advice and training so that he could realistically aspire to future promotion.

10.6   Appointment of managers

The health service does not have a good record of performance appraisal and management development. In many cases we could train and prepare staff with potential for promotion so that they can readily step into jobs. Managers in private industry are groomed for promotion and they do not have to face interview panels who can make arbitrary judgements. Senior management is going to be forced to tackle this complex issue of management succession. Similar issues need to be addressed when first line supervisors are appointed.

First level supervisors nowadays have to cope with budgets, works requisitions and a complex bureaucracy. A strong plea is made for proper support and counselling together with first level training which must cover staff management issues, instead of just expecting a new supervisor to cope.

In the case study both a new works manager and two new supervisors were appointed. In the case of the supervisors a query over equal opportunities was raised. The appointment or promotion of staff is clearly a time when there is an opportunity to change style. Was it possible that macho managers were promoted?

Before making appointments any manager needs to have a clear specification. In the past perhaps we have promoted the best craftsman, the best nurse or the most articulate administrator. Good technical skills are important, but what we really need are management skills which will be identified and fostered only with proper planning and care.

10.7 Equal opportunities

There has been equal opportunities legislation in the UK for over 10 years. Efforts have been made to increase openings for ethnic minorities, but UK legislation has not required managers to discriminate positively in favour of minority groups to the extent that legislation has in other countries. Some local councils have taken this step and it is certainly a possibility for the future. In the US, legislation has gone much further and large organisations are required to have affirmative action plans. They are also more open to be sued by individuals who take a 'class action' against them.

This means that an individual sues on behalf of him or herself together with others similarly affected. Multi-million dollar settlements have been paid and US organisations are having to make certain that their minority groups are moving up the management ladder. In the UK we must expect to promote more women to senior management posts if we are to meet the spirit of the legislation. In many health authorities there are three times as many women as men but the ratio is not yet reflected in the senior positions. The same criticism could be levelled at the promotion of other minority groups.

Equal opportunities is a complex subject. Sometimes it becomes purely associated with race or sex, but the legislation and the spirit of policies is much wider and we all need to be aware of this. We need to consider colour, creed, sexuality, disability, marital status, age and nationality.

Senior management must take a firm line on equal opportunities if further difficulties are to be prevented. In the case study the problem was smoothed over but, if the unit works manager had tackled the issue, perhaps the violence which occurred later might have been avoided. Some managers are good at smoothing things over or keeping the lid on situations and this can become a habit. There are arguments both ways but continually to avoid problems can and does store up trouble for the future.

10.8   Contractors

Comment was also made about the use of contractors. The strikes which occurred in early 1988 in Scotland in the NHS were against the policy of contracting out.

However, as cost pressures grow it is likely that more authorities will increasingly use contractors, and it seems probable that this will result in further conflict. There is no doubt that at times money can be saved by contracting work out, but there are other positive arguments which tend to get overlooked. Amongst these are:

- The health service is short of good managers and requires them to manage a very wide range of activity. At times specialist organisations concentrating on one particular field can produce better managers and results
- A lot of authorities and commercial organisations use contractors to meet peak work requirements whilst retaining the base load for their own staff
- At times contractors can recruit more easily because they have flexibility of payrates. They can be more productive because they can use their workforce more flexibly. They can also at times afford to spend more on training their staff
- In some organisations, where labour relations are poor, management have quite deliberately chosen to contract work out. The advantage at the end of a contract is that it is easy to bring in a new contractor but it is much more difficult to change your own workforce

There are many other arguments in favour of contractors including better purchasing skills, but a manager does need to think through the situation carefully before making a commitment which is likely to alienate the existing workforce. Contractors mean less security and stability and are seen as a threat by the workforce – a threat that may lead to stoppages.

10.9 What could the unit manager have done?

Earlier in the chapter some comments were made on the way in which works departments are organised. The UGM needed also to know more about the workforce; for example the age profile and the level of sickness absence. A recent calculation in one works department showed that the charge-out rates had to be increased by 8p per hour for every 1 per cent increase in sickness absence. High sickness absence can reflect low morale and poor supervision. Surprisingly there is no published health service data on sickness absence, so it is not easy to give comparative data. In one works department strenuous efforts are being made to reduce the level of absence from 15 per cent to 5 per cent. Controlling sickness absence should be a target for any manager since very significant costs can be incurred.

Similarly, control over timekeeping is very important. However, while exercising control in these areas, the manager is not necessarily going to promote a high level of motivation among the workforce. In the case study, one major problem was the failure of communication. By involving the workforce and gaining their interest and support, much more could have been achieved than by the autocratic approach that was used.

Over 20 years ago a management team faced with a similar problem in industry decided to make a presentation about alleged poor performance to a maintenance department of over 700 craftsmen. They hired a cinema, transported the staff there in a fleet of buses and gave a presentation highlighting various indicators which compared performance on a world wide basis. The evidence was that productivity was poor. At the end of the presentations the senior shop steward got to his feet and remarked that he was a very keen soccer supporter. He went on to explain that in a professional soccer club the manager would have got the sack first and he expected that to happen in this case. It was good humoured, but the rest of his team got the message!

There are very many methods of getting messages across. Several health authorities use team briefing techniques to help get messages from senior managers to their staff and back. Others have started to use quality circles to encourage staff to pull together and solve problems jointly. A number of foreign based companies have helped spread the idea of regular 10-minute briefings on work plans, usually at the start of a day.

Other managers have tried different techniques of communicating and involving their workforce. Some, like Sir Michael Edwardes in British Leyland, appealed directly over the heads of junior managers and unions to get his message across. Others have involved union officials, newspapers, videos, noticeboards.

It should have been in the interest of the workforce in the case study to take note of management concerns, and managers should have capitalised on their material concern. The men would not like to lose work to contractors if they could avoid it. The trade union officials would probably much prefer to deal with health service managers rather than contractors and frequently can be very helpful in creating change situations – for example, union officials do support the introduction of well constructed bonus schemes which tie pay to productivity. It is better to highlight points where manager and staff can work together rather than conflict areas.

A technique which managers sometimes use is to employ consultants. In fact ACAS have a good deal of consultancy experience but the health service also uses commercial management consultants widely. One of the advantages is that they usually have broad experience and can draw on considerable databases. Clearly, unions can be suspicious and consultants need to be introduced carefully, but they can be of significant value and are looked on as third parties.

All managers and supervisors have a feedback role; they are the leaders and do need to give guidance and support. Many managers are too diffident in reviewing performance, but they should recognize this as an essential part of their role. In the sporting field, leading sportsmen employ coaches and managers to help improve their performance – an analogy that could equally apply to the health service. Managers also need to take a keen interest in training. Mention has already been made of management training but members of a workforce will equally benefit from training. Many craftsmen will have completed an apprenticeship years ago and their skills may no longer be consistent with current practice. Large service organisations invest time and effort in this area so that they know that their workforce is using up to date techniques. There are many inexpensive ways of achieving this and regular questions need to be asked at a senior level about this aspect of work.

Clearly accepted policies and procedures provide a sound basis for discussion. Employment policies can be bureaucratic and out of date. On the other hand they can provide a framework which may limit maverick action. In the case study, the authority disputes procedure should have been used and it would have been necessary to apply equal opportunities procedures. Others, such as new technology agreements, AIDS employment policies, sickness absence and alcohol abuse will have to be used on different occasions. A forward looking personnel department should work with managers to anticipate policy requirements and to maintain up to date procedures and policies. It is easy for policies to become out of date and hence inadequate when required. Managers have a clear responsibility to ensure that this does not happen.

On a more general note, all managers must continually be searching for productivity improvements. It is possible that the unit works group had become ossified. Perhaps in the health service, with its continuous flow of clients, guaranteed income and inadequate performance indicators, we may have been complacent in the past. British industry has, in recent years, been subject to a blast of competition and this has caused many changes. Sometimes the changes have, perforce, been dramatic but a better approach must be to look for productivity improvements on a continuous basis, setting targets to be met by the workforce.

10.10 Summary

The thrust behind introducing the new style 'Griffiths' management was to have a much more professional management. This clearly has implications for the workforce whether staff have a clinical training or not. As performance related pay is introduced further down the structure, increased emphasis will be placed on cost control, productivity and the achievement of targets. There is going to be pressure at national level for work to be contracted out.

In this situation, how is a manager to react to the industrial relations scene? The case study highlighted points where managers were attempting to make progress, consequently riding roughshod over objections, failing to communicate and perhaps not looking for change in a consistent manner. Good labour relations requires considerable care, thought and long term planning. Good clear communications in both directions are essential. The involvement and the cooperation of the workforce should be sought. Local stewards have a role to play, but clearly it is wrong to rely on them or their union officials to generate change. Managers have to be seen to take a lead and must not become cut off from the workforce. It is not always possible to effect the changes required at the speed some senior managers want and this needs to be explained to them. They need to understand that the successful completion of negotiations is a time consuming business.

The clear evidence, however, is that by working with and involving staff, more progress will be made and stoppages as described in the case study are much less likely.

Bibliography

ACAS Various publications, advisory booklets, 11–12 St James Square, London SW1Y 4LA.

G. Bain, *Industrial Relations in Britain* (Oxford: Blackwell, 1983).

Commission for Racial Equality, various publications, booklets and advisory service, 11–12 St James Square, London SW1Y 4LA.

Department of Employment, Central Office of Industrial Tribunals, *Industrial Tribunals Procedure* (London: HMSO, 1986).

L. Dickens, *et al.*, *Dismissed* (Oxford: Blackwell, 1985).

Equal Opportunities Commission, *Equality at work* (and various other publications) Overseas House, Quay Street, Manchester, M3 3HN.

M. Goodman, *Industrial Tribunals Practice and Procedure*, (London: Sweet and Maxwell, 1987).

S. Harrison, *Hearing Disciplinary Appeals* (Birmingham: National Association of Health Authorities, 1983).

Industrial Relations Service, *Equal Opportunities Review*, published 6 times per year, 18–20 Highbury Place, London N5 1QP

King Edward's Hospital Fund, *Equal Opportunities Policy* (Kings Fund Task Force 1987) Industrial Relations with the NHS (London: King's Fund, 1987).

11
Capital Planning and Commissioning
Isobel Curry

11.1 Introduction

Capital planning is the process by which new or upgraded buildings are developed. Commissioning is the process in which the completed building is equipped and brought into use.

Before a building is planned, the need for it must be demonstrated. The idea will evolve from strategic planning, based on national, regional and district policies, which demonstrate the service needs. Since it is not always necessary to provide new buildings to meet these needs, an option appraisal exercise is carried out.

Option appraisal looks at all the ways which may be available for providing the service. If the best solution is to build new accommodation, the content of the scheme will be defined and costed. A project team will be appointed and a brief drawn up for the design team. The project team will be responsible for ensuring that the building is completed within the programme dates and within the money allocated. Revenue costs must be assessed and the source of funding identified.

The design team will produce a series of plans for the project team to agree. The plans will vary from a rough layout to carefully drawn scale plans which the contractor will use. It will not always be possible to build what the users want, as site availability and money may act as constraints.

An understanding of the procedures to be followed and the guidance issued by the Department of Health will help reach a satisfactory solution and also save time.

When the scheme has been designed and the costs have been

agreed, the contractor will be appointed and building will begin. After completion it will be commissioned for use and evaluated when fully operational for at least six months.

11.2   Case study: development of Maplewood district hospital

This district had its acute services scattered over four different sites. Many were in poor buildings and were of inadequate size. It was necessary to improve the existing services, increase the number of acute beds, centralise both the surgical facilities and the accident and emergency departments.

The money available in the regional capital programme was restricted, so the redevelopment had to be phased over a number of years.

An option appraisal exercise was carried out to help decide which site to use, and the services to be provided in the various phases.

The area available on the preferred site was restricted. However, the rehabilitation department was occupying a prime part of the site and was in poor single storey accommodation. Although not high on the list of priorities for replacement, it was decided to incorporate a new rehabilitation department as part of the first phase development to maximise the use of the site. A project team was therefore formed to develop the scheme in accordance with Capricode guidance.

The name Capricode will crop up frequently when referring to capital schemes. It is the procedure guide issued by the Department of Health and provides a logical sequence of stages to ensure the satisfactory completion of a capital scheme. Its use in planning capital schemes is mandatory.

11.3   Approval in Principle

An Approval in Principle submission (AIP) must be made for every capital scheme costing more than £250000. For schemes up to £10 million approval can be given by the regional health authority. Schemes over £10 million require approval from the

Department of Health and if the scheme is more than £15 million, then Treasury approval is required.

Optional appraisal is an integral part of the AIP, since no capital scheme can proceed without it.

The AIP will consist of:

● A summary of the option appraisal within the strategic planning context
● The service and development objectives including the performance criteria for the various options
● A list of the options considered and reasons for rejection
● An evaluation of the options with a description of the preferred option and justification for its selection
● A description of the proposed scheme, giving the functional content, proposed site, estimated capital costs, and the estimated running costs, and the programme for carrying out the redevelopment

11.4   Option appraisal

The first part of providing the new building was an option appraisal exercise. Facilities on several sites were not only expensive to run, but did not provide a satisfactory service for patients.

All possible options were identified and appraisal of them demonstrated that a capital scheme was necessary. All buildings in the district were in poor condition, and the site chosen was central to the users and was large enough for future developments.

The aim in an option appraisal exercise is to ensure that before a specific solution is adopted, authorities understand the issues to be resolved and the objectives to be pursued. The respective advantages and disadvantages of each option must be recognised, and at the end of the exercise it must be demonstrated that the preferred option is value for money.

When undertaking an option appraisal exercise it is important to examine honestly all the options available and not to start with a preconceived idea of what the solution will be.

11.5   Formulation of options

It is useful to 'brainstorm' in order to put forward possible solutions and ensure that ideas are not missed. An appraisal team of all disciplines from the district and some representatives from the region was established.

This team put forward every solution which came to mind even if some appeared farfetched and impossible. Ideas were generated which were then discussed. Some were discarded and others considered in greater detail, to determine their value.

- Was it necessary to build everything new?
- Were there any departments which could be upgraded?
- As money was limited, what were the most important departments to build in the first phase?

In proposing the options to be examined it was necessary to know the service options which were available. Could the service be provided by day care or community care? Where should the new building be sited, and when could the scheme be implemented?

It is important that in examining the various suggestions, the option to do nothing, or a minimum redevelopment, must be considered. At Maplewood District the 'do nothing' option demonstrated that it was expensive to retain the rehabilitation and outpatient departments which were in buildings of poor quality and were expensive to run. The outpatient department was in an ideal position for the accident and emergency department and, therefore, if a new outpatient department was provided, the old building could be converted for A & E use.

Having established a large number of options, a preliminary sift was carried out to reduce the options to a manageable number.

Options were considered because:

- They satisfied the objectives
- They did not violate constraints in terms of finances, manpower, site and building availability

A shortlist was drawn up and the characteristics of each option described.

In assessing the various options a number of questions must be posed.

- What are the benefits?
- What are the capital costs?
- What are the revenue costs?
- Why do the costs differ for the various options?
- Is funding available – both capital and revenue?

The content of the first phase was finally agreed to contain:

1. Outpatients department.
2. Rehabilitation.
3. Surgical wards.
4. Intensive care unit.
5. Operating department.
6. Catering facilities for staff and patients.

The existing outpatients department will be converted to the accident and emergency department on completion of the scheme. As the works cost was over £10 million, approval was needed from the Department of Health.

11.6 The preferred option

The preferred option was presented to the district health authority for approval.

The relative advantages and disadvantages in relation to the option appraisal objectives and the district strategic plan were explained.

They included the following details:

- The benefits of the scheme – an improved and more convenient service for the users
- The capital costs of the scheme including building and equipment costs and the assumed life of the buildings
- The estimated annual running costs broken down into staff and non staff groups together with the components of these

groups – for example nursing staff salaries and the cost of cleaning the building
- Discounted capital costs – large undertakings require planning and the costs are spread over a number of years. By applying a discount rate converting future monetary sums to their equivalent value in today's terms, the present value of costs and benefits to be met in the future is established. The discount rate is the rate at which the present value of a future £, in real terms, falls away through time. By discounting, all options can be compared on an equal basis
- The implications of any sensitivity analysis – this means varying the capital or revenue costs by a specific percentage and examining the effect on the conclusions – for example the nursing costs for a particular option may be 10 per cent higher or lower than other options and these costs may determine which option is chosen
- The implications that the recommendation may have on existing and future service provision – in this case further phases of development will be essential to meet the service needs of the district

Other factors which should be considered, but were not relevant in this case are:

- Any non NHS costs, such as a contribution from the local authority, or any private donations
- Land costs – will land need to be purchased, or will any land be released for sale?
- Funding implications and effects on other health authorities – will the new building alter patient flows in neighbouring districts?

11.7 Costs

Capital costs consist of:

- Building costs
- Land purchase if required
- Professional fees
- Equipment

The Department of Health allows a specific sum of money for each ward or department, and no increase can be allowed. These costs are known as the departmental cost allowances (DCAs).

11.7.1 Building costs

These are arrived at by using departmental cost allowances and on-costs. Departmental costs are the costs allowed for a specific unit, and the on-costs are the costs required to build a scheme on a specific site. It is mandatory to work within the appropriate departmental cost allowances, but on-costs vary according to the chosen site. At the beginning of an appraisal exercise on-costs are reflected as a percentage of the DCAs but in determining the preferred option a realistic assessment of on-costs for each scheme must be made.

11.7.2 Professional fees

Professional fees are those paid to the design team members, such as architect, engineers – mechanical, electrical and structural – and quantity surveyors. The services of a landscape architect and interior designer were also required.

Although there are scale fees recommended by the various professional bodies of design consultants, fees for a scheme should be obtained either by competition or negotiation with the suitable design consultants.

11.7.3 Equipment costs

Such costs are based on the functional content of each scheme and equipment cost allowances are allocated on the same basis as DCAs. There is a specific cost per unit. Frequently a new capital scheme is equipped totally with new equipment, and insufficient attention is paid to transferring existing equipment which may still be usable.

11.8 Management teams

After the option appraisal was completed and the scheme and its content agreed by the DHA, RHA and DoH, a project team was set up.

11.8.1   Project team

This was a multidisciplinary team consisting of district, regional and design team representatives. The team should be as small as possible and be capable of making decisions without reference to others.

Responsibility for managing the scheme to ensure its completion within time and cost limits was vested in one person, the project manager. The project team was responsible for producing the brief for the design team.
The brief consisted of:

● Operational policies for individual departments
● Operational policies which relate to the function of services for the whole hospital. No design work should be undertaken until all the operational policies are complete. They are the foundation of a scheme
● Schedules of accommodation – these list the various rooms in a department and state the size of each room
● Room data sheets which describe the function and content of each room

The work of the project team involved the use of standard information which is readily available. It is not necessary to reinvent the wheel for each project. Personal idiosyncracies must be avoided. Those who are involved in the early stages of planning have invariably moved on by the time the scheme is up and running.

11.8.2   Working groups

Working groups relating to the various departments which would be built were set up, and it was at this level that users were involved in planning their units. Decisions made by the working groups were ratified by the project team.

11.8.3   Design team

The key members were the architect, engineer and quantity surveyor.

The architect designed the building, engineers designed the structure and the electrical and mechanical services, while the quantity surveyor was responsible for costing the scheme and advising on the cost control.

The architect was also responsible for leading, controlling, and ensuring the efficient, harmonious working of the team. Drawings had to be produced according to the programme to allow time for the quantity surveyor to do the costings.

The design team was chosen by selecting firms which were known to be capable of carrying out the required work satisfactorily, and inviting them to submit a fee bid.

11.9   Design state

Over the years, a systemised building development has evolved, known as Nucleus. This consists of a series of cruciform templates which can be linked together. Each template contains about 1000 square metres of space, can be stacked two and, in some cases, three storeys high and can be linked by a hospital street.

If a Nucleus solution can be used, then considerable time will be save in briefing the design team, resulting in an earlier start on site.

Many departments have been planned in these templates and each project team, before deciding its building solution, must explore the use of the Nucleus scheme and, if they reject it, must give reasons. At Maplewood the available site was not large enough to allow a low level development, but future phases of the hospital will incorporate the Nucleus designs.

The design brief was finalised in accordance with the information previously agreed. Room data sheets were produced and more detailed larger scale plans developed.

Room data sheets were completed by the project team or user groups, describing the function of each room, the furniture and equipment needed, the services required, such as socket outlets and piped medical gases and the environment (is mechanical ventilation required?). The architect then produced drawings to a larger scale, usually 1:50, which demonstrated the contents and layout of the room.

Plans may not be easily understood, particularly the various scales which are used. Members of the design team may speak a technical language which is not understood by other members of the project team. Every member of a project team should be able to understand the total design process, and if they are not clear about what is being discussed, or cannot understand the plans, then must say so. Architects can always make plans comprehensible.

It may be difficult to appreciate size, so it is always useful to know the areas and measurements of one or two familiar rooms, which will help understand areas in the schedule of accommodation. A schedule of 10 square metres may be meaningless, but if it can be visualised as a room 10 feet by 10 feet, a better understanding of space will result.

At each stage of planning the brief was frozen. When the small scale plans for a department showing room sizes and room relationships were agreed, no further alterations were allowed. There could be no going back, as it was essential for the design team to proceed with more detailed work. The programme must be adhered to and, as the design team have all the detailed design to carry out, users must not change their minds. This causes delays and delays cost money.

Once the plans and room data sheets were agreed by the project team, the design team produced the working drawings. These are the detailed plans to which the contractor will work. Very little input from the project team is needed during this period.

As the design proceeded, local planning authorities were consulted. If there had been any land transactions they would have been dealt with after approval of the AIP. Cost control was maintained throughout this period with regular design and cost reports prepared for the project manager. A budget cost was finally agreed for the scheme. This meant that no increase in costs could be allowed for any reason, therefore no changes could be made to the scheme if they had a cost implication.

11.10 Pre-tender and tender stage

When the design of the scheme was complete, the quantity

surveyor estimated its cost and prepared the tender documents which would allow contractors to bid for the work.

At the pre-tender and tender stage the costs were higher than the agreed budget cost. The scheme was re-examined before going out to tender and savings made. When these tenders were returned the price was over the adjusted pre-tender estimate and discussions took place between the client and the contractor to see if further savings could be made without reducing the specifications. After these adjustments were made, approval was obtained for some increase in cost. The increase over the estimated cost reflected rising costs in the building industry.

11.11 Construction

As with the appointment of design consultants, contractors who were considered capable of building the scheme were invited to tender.

All the plans, bills of quantities and specifications were sent to the contractors who, within a given period and on a specific date, submitted their bids for the scheme.

The tender was awarded to the contractor who could meet the specifications of design, price and time, and building began.

During the contract period, the site is the builder's property and health service staff should not visit. No orders or changes must be given to the contractor. Only the project manager can authorise any instructions during the construction time.

Some alterations may be deemed necessary because of changes in statutory regulations or modern technology. Alterations should not be allowed during the building period, since changes in the instructions given to the contractor could allow him to claim extra money. Any extra works that are essential should be carried out during the commissioning period. These are known as post contract variations.

Finally, the building was completed to the satisfaction of the project manager and was handed over for commissioning.

11.12   Commissioning

Commissioning means bringing a new building into use – a time-consuming and complicated business for a major project.
  Essential for commissioning are:

- A commissioning team
- Equipment schedules
- A programme of all events
- Transfer of services

11.12.1   *The commissioning team*

A team consisting of a manager, a nurse, a doctor and an equipment officer was appointed as soon as the tender was let. Although the project was managed by regional staff, commissioning is the district's responsibility and they appointed the team. Its role was to prepare the building for use according to the brief and policies formulated during the early stages of planning. The policies were expanded to produce operational manuals which described in detail how each ward, department and service would function.

11.12.2   *Equipment schedules*

During the planning stages furniture and equipment had been identified on the room data sheets only as objects needing space. Now was the time to specify exactly what was wanted and place orders for delivery.
  Some items of equipment need to be ordered many months in advance to achieve the desired delivery date. Savings could also be made by bulk buying. Storage space is always at a premium, so delivery of the equipment had to be programmed to minimise storage problems and also avoid double handling where possible. In this case, a new divisional stores had just been completed so storage was no problem.
  The equipment officer produced lists of equipment relevant for each ward and department, and agreed with users the make to be ordered.
  All equipment was checked on arrival to ensure that what had

been ordered was delivered and that it was not damaged. Where items were subject to warranty, arrangements were made with the supplier to make certain that the warranty started on the date on which the item was brought into use, and not on the day that it was delivered.

11.12.3 Programming

Throughout this period everything associated with the commissioning was programmed. The contractor's date for completion was the most important date, and everything revolved around that date. Would it finish on time or not? Also included in the programme was the training of staff to prepare them for work in new departments. In a development as large as this, wards and departments were moved in sequence and this also was programmed.

11.12.4 Transfer of services

The building was finally handed over on the planned date and transfer of services began. First of all the catering services were brought into use, the outpatients and rehabilitation departments were next, and finally, patients were transferred to the new wards.

Although the operating department had been handed over, there were problems with the ventilation plant and several weeks passed before the defects were ironed out and the plant was working satisfactorily.

The first few months were very traumatic for the staff. They had to familiarise themselves with their new surroundings, and the multibay wards with all the necessary facilities were quite a contrast to the old, inadequate Nightingale wards they had been used to. Inevitably there were teething problems and some things did not work as planned. Shelving in treatment rooms was inadequate, and in the very early days the fire alarms went off frequently.

After about six months everything including the theatre plant was working satisfactorily. In addition to the commissioning of the wards and departments, engineers from the construction company were also busy commissioning the engineering plant and training the hospital works staff.

The commissioning team was involved in presenting the new facilities to the public who would be using them. Publicity about the building was produced and circulated, and arrangements made for interested parties to visit. All visits were controlled and coordinated by the commissioning team. These visits were very successful and the public quickly identified with the new buildings. All patients, the public and the staff are delighted with their new surroundings.

During commissioning it is important to remember that the building was planned to a specific brief with specific policies and should be used in the way it was planned. The commissioning period should not be used as an excuse to change the planning principles.

Eventually the new building was running satisfactorily and an opening ceremony was arranged.

11.13   Evaluation

Evaluation takes place in two ways:

1. Continuously during the planning stages. Notes should be made at each stage on the success of the briefing material, the design and the cost control. Each project manager should relay comments to a reference point coordinating evaluation reports.
2. After the building has been fully operational for six months to one year. A multi-disciplinary team consisting of the users, design and planning experts should examine whether or not the building is performing as expected.

The items to be evaluated will be:

- The adequacy of the space provided
- The standard of fittings and finishes
- The quality of the building
- The performance of the plant
- User opinions – staff and patients

Evaluation is based on the planning brief. A unit that functions in a manner which differs significantly from the operational policies cannot then be evaluated against a redundant planning brief.

11.14   Conclusion

Planning and building capital schemes can be long and tedious. Frequently, when a building is open there are few people around who were involved in its planning, and this was the case in Maplewood.

It is essential, therefore, that those who are involved in planning buildings understand the need for adequate briefing. Operational policies should be carefully thought out and care given to the way the service will function.

If an optional appraisal exercise has been carried out satisfactorily, the brief made clear to the design team, and the project managed satisfactorily, complaints about a new building should be avoided. Members of the project team should understand their role and be aware of all the guidance material which is available.

Time spent on the early stages of a project preparing the brief generally ensures a smooth running scheme and a building in which patients will feel comfortable and staff will enjoy working.

Bibliography

Department of Health. *Optional Appraisal. A guide for the National Health Service* (London: HMSO, 1987).
Department of Health. *Capricode. Health Building Procedures* (London: HMSO, 1986).
Department of Health and the Welsh Office. *Health Building Notes and Design Briefing Systems* (London: HMSO).
Department of Health. *Health Buildings Evaluation Manual* (London: HMSO, 1987).
Graham Millard, *Commissioning Hospital Buildings. A King's Fund Guide* (London: King's Fund, 1981).

12
Making Changes Happen
Laurie McMahon with Suzanne Goodband

12.1 Introduction

Perhaps the first question we should ask is why have a chapter about managing change at all? After all, the preceding chapters all deal with managers attempting either to alter systems or structures or to get people to behave differently. It could be said that change is really what management is all about – in which case, why the special chapter?

In one way it is a convention. Most management textbooks have chapters on managing change, and most self-respecting management courses have sessions on 'change management'. Yet this convention has grown out of the real concerns of practising managers, and those concerns must mean that 'making changes happen' is not something that managers find particularly easy. Maybe one reason for the difficulty is the way managers have been taught to think about management, in that the conventional wisdom about what managers do, and how organisations work, actually prevents managers from understanding the change process properly.

When talking about ideas for this chapter with a nurse who is now a district general manager, she remarked that it was interesting that ward sisters seem to be well able to influence the behaviour of others involved in the work of the ward – managing change (albeit on a relatively small scale) – by using commonsense tactics. Yet somehow, after they have been 'processed' through the management training machine and proceed to senior management positions a great deal of that basic *nous* seems to be schooled out of them. It is substituted by a 'management think'; a tutored naivety, that hampers rather than helps them to make changes happen.

If there is any truth in that, then there are good reasons to examine conventional management thinking to see if there may be alternative ideas that can help us better understand, and therefore better manage, the change process.

From the conventional perspective, organisations exist to achieve specific goals. Indeed, that is the way most writers differentiate between organisations and other social groupings. They are seen as machines; social machines built for a purpose or goal but with people instead of parts. The 'parts' in the social machine have their functions prescribed by job descriptions and task specifications, and are arranged in hierarchical authority structures.

These, together with sets of policies and procedures, ensure that individual efforts mesh in such a way that departmental functions are carried out, and that each department's efforts slot together to ensure that the organisation's goal is achieved. Obviously, we have caricatured this view, but before dismissing it out of hand as too unrealistic, just think about the hierarchical structures, the job descriptions, the procedures and so on, upon which much of the management in your organisation is built. Even if you *know* that health care is not like a machine, much of the management systems and structures are designed as if it were.

The machine model implies that once the prime goal is identified and the appropriate structures and processes are established to achieve it, then change should be something out of the ordinary. Moreover, it also implies that making organisations work, or changing them if they do not, is a simple business; just a matter of deciding what needs to be done differently and then reprogramming the machine. This is done by restructuring roles or rewriting departmental policies, or redefining operational procedures and job descriptions and the like.

Expressed like this, it is dismaying when, on occasion, we find it impossible to introduce the most rational of solutions to the most obvious of problems. However, while it would be nice if the organisational machine could be rearranged in this mechanical way, maybe the real world is not as conventional management thinking would have us believe.

To explore this idea further, perhaps we should turn away

from the orthodox prescriptions and think a little more carefully about our everyday working experience. To do this, we will use a case study that will help us see the management of change in a somewhat different light.

12.2 Case study

This case study is about changes in the way patient services are managed and technical advice utilised, on the wards of a 100-bed paediatric unit. Given the issues involved, it is important to note that the events took place well before the 1988 clinical grading review.

Ruth, the assistant director of nursing services at the unit, had been unhappy about the way in which two nursing officers related to the trained staff of the hospital. They were both extremely experienced. The younger had recently run a big 'state of the art' intensive care unit (ICU) and the other, a more mature woman, had been appointed because she was felt to be extremely level headed and had 'seen it all before'.

However, Ruth had an impression that the clinical and managerial experience of these nursing officers was not being drawn on by the trained staff. This general impression was confirmed by two incidents. The first involved Ruth finding a junior doctor and sister pouring over a textbook reading up on a child's condition. What troubled Ruth was that the nursing officer on duty had particular experience in such cases, but that this was not being used by the sister.

The second incident involved a mother who complained to Ruth that the sister would not listen to her concerns about a change in her son's treatment. The sister had obviously become caught between a well intentioned doctor and an articulate parent, but the nursing officer, with all her experience, had not been involved earlier to help resolve what had now become a formal complaint.

This state of affairs was not good enough, since the nursing officers were employed to provide clinical support and advice. Ruth was concerned that the quality of patient care could be much improved if there was some way in which the nursing officers' experience could be better utilised.

Ruth set about dealing with these issues by chatting to the nursing officers, the sisters and the doctors, to try to get a better picture of what was going on.

The ward sisters, identifying closely with their consultants on the ward, saw the nursing officers as outsiders, useful as a source of agency staff (and even as relief staff in an emergency) but not as a source of clinical support. They felt that it was almost a criticism of their professional judgement and experience if they had to call on this 'external' help. They said that they would gain a reputation for not having the required experience to run the ward. They also said that the doctors would not accept having patient care 'interfered with' by management.

The doctors seemed to view the nursing officers as part of the 'hospital bureaucracy' – people totally separate from patient care who restricted their access to beds from time to time. They also perceived clinical advice from the nursing officers as a challenge to their own clinical authority.

The nursing officers had sensed all this and found that, after trying to provide clinical support for a while, they 'gave in' and reverted to worrying about the more managerial aspects of their jobs.

After thinking over her problem, Ruth felt that there seemed to be at least three courses of possible action:

● Option 1 was to accept that the nurses and doctors on the ward would not take clinical advice from nursing officers. She would therefore appoint a deputy to help manage the unit, and do without the nursing officers. This at least would mean that Ruth was not paying for unused expertise. It would be an easy change to introduce, since it would re-establish the accepted practice. Furthermore, it would be endorsed, perhaps actively welcomed, by the doctors and nurses who would be rid of what they felt to be interference. There was not even a problem in 'disposing' of the existing nursing officers, since the one with ICU experience was getting frustrated and was applying for jobs elsewhere, while the other would make a good deputy. However, this option would tend to centralise management decision-making and leave little opportunity for clinical advice to be given or for the professional development of the nurses. Nor did Ruth like the feeling of being beaten by custom and practice

● Option 2 was to work with the sisters and doctors, explaining to them how the experience of nursing officers could be used and encouraging the nursing officers to push harder into the clinical work of the wards. This would involve a great deal of persuasion, and would produce many opportunities for open conflict. Ruth was also worried that she should not tell people to 'do better' while leaving the real cause of the problem unresolved

● Option 3 was to recognise the strength of the relationship between consultants and ward sisters and to accept that external advisory relationships were difficult. The best way to introduce a strong clinical support function into the wards was probably to appoint a 'super sister' for each ward who would have this as a key part of her role, and to jettison the nursing officers altogether. This idea was not entirely original, since she had heard at a conference about a similar experiment being tried in another hospital. They had found that the clinical support role worked very well and that there were also marked advantages in devolving management from the nursing officer to the wards

Ruth realised that it was the ideal solution to the core problem, but that it would be a nightmare to put into place. It involved fairly radical changes to working arrangements and could be resisted by the sisters, the doctors, Ruth's superiors and many other people who were used to the convention of having nursing officers in the unit.

It was at this stage that Ruth learnt that her potential deputy had become pregnant and intended to leave, and that the other nursing officer had been successful in gaining a more clinically orientated job elsewhere. This meant that in three or four months' time she would have to do something, but she was beginning to get nervous about the implementation of her ideal solution.

Let us leave the story there for a moment to consider its implications so far.

12.3 Issues

There is nothing unusual about the case; it is an everyday story of nurse management, but notice how sharply it contrasts with the prescriptions of our orthodox model of change management. Ruth knows that she has the managerial authority to make these changes, but she also knows that she is dependent on a large number of people in the system to make the changes happen. She realises that she has not the power to force people to accept the changes and make them work in a way that she desires.

So the people involved, the junior doctors and the nurses, are not passive parts of the machine waiting to be restructured or reprogrammed. Instead, either as individuals or groups, they seem to have an agenda of their own – a set of interests that they will pursue. It is as if each group has its own goals which may or, equally likely, may not mesh with those of the manager.

In place of the consensual, coordinated, goal–driven view of the orthodox approach, we now have a picture in which organisations seem more like arenas for conflict, where a number of partisans are busy negotiating around an issue, all attempting to advance their interests in the way it is resolved.

If this is correct, then perhaps we should think again about the nature of managerial authority. If people do not respond compliantly to a manager's right to manage, then the manager is not 'in control' as we usually imagine, but instead may only be able to influence outcomes to a greater or lesser extent.

So, instead of being seen as the captain of a well ordered and purposeful ship, managers may be better seen as wrestling with a large number of powerful stakeholders, attempting to produce outcomes that best meet their own interests and needs. This 'micro-political' or 'power-bargaining' perspective represents an alternative to the orthodox view of organisational life, that may provide a more accurate description of the real world in which we work. It says something different about the management of change too.

The 'status quo' does not exist because the manager has decreed it, but because it has been negotiated. It is the outcome of a bargaining process, and that outcome is determined by the number of partisans involved, the nature of their interests in the issue, and the relative strength of their bargaining power. The manager is one of the partisans who can change outcomes by increasing or decreasing the number of partisans, altering the nature of their interests or by doing something about the relative strength of their bargaining power.

Even though this may involve the manager using the power of her or his position, this is rather different from our earlier assumption that the management of change is simply a matter of identifying the ideal solution and then using the prerogative!

Let us return to the case study and examine the issues involved in negotiating change.

12.4 Case study (continued)

Ruth began to think through how her preferred solution of appointing senior sisters into the wards could be implemented. It seemed to be a tangled web of uncertainty and guesswork.

The sisters might like the extra autonomy, but would they want the extra responsibility? Even if Ruth appointed nurses with the right sort of clinical experience to the 'super sister' role, would they be resisted by the other sisters?

The doctors, having seen so many reorganisations of nursing hierarchies, might not be interested in the proposed changes. However, if they were, they might upset everything by refusing to recognise the senior sisters and by coming directly to Ruth with issues previously handled by the nursing officers. Moreover, the consultants might respond to the sisters' dissatisfaction and even use the division of paediatrics to oppose the changes or, worse, talk to the district general manager or chief nursing officer and ask them to intervene in an informal way.

It was obvious that Ruth would have to talk to each of the parties involved to detect how they might respond to the changes, and to see if she could find ways of making the changes advantageous to them.

The first thing Ruth did was to clear the ground with the director of nursing services (DNS). She was sceptical, and doubted if the fuss of making the changes was worthwhile. She felt that there were enough problems at the moment without stirring up another contentious issue. She would probably have resisted the change altogether had Ruth not also explained the problem of continuing to provide a service whilst attempting to recruit two high quality nursing officers at the same time. The DNS, almost as a solution to the recruitment problem, then agreed that it was worth a try.

Next, Ruth talked to the four sisters whom she wished to recruit into the senior sister posts. She explained what would be expected of them and the nature of the support she would give during the early stages of the project. They too were cautious, particularly about the reaction of the other sisters, but they recognised that promotion was involved and also felt they could do much to improve the standard of nursing care. They thought that they would be better able to manage the doctors when the focal point for managing nursing care was on the wards.

Ruth then turned to the doctors. She had a good relationship with the chairman of the division and met him informally to explain the predicament. She emphasised that the changes would mean less interference from outside the ward, and that quicker decisions about bed availability could result from having the nurses responsible for allocations on the wards. Generally accepting the argument, the chairman offered to put the issue on the division's agenda so that Ruth could discuss it with his colleagues. Knowing the sensitivity of the bed use issue, she let it be known during the meeting that if her proposals were not implemented, a possible consequence was that bed utilisation would be centrally managed from her office.

Towards the end of the meeting, the chairman raised a seemingly unrelated issue. He suggested that one of the problems on the wards was the lack of office space for medical students, and asked what would be happening to the redundant nursing officers' office. Ruth felt that in an oblique way she was being offered what was tantamount to a deal.

Apart from these 'set piece' meetings, Ruth spent a great deal of time talking informally, using every opportunity to dispel anxieties and extol the potential gains to be made from the changes. She also worked closely with the nursing officers to prevent them feeling 'redundant' whilst still carrying out their important functions.

When one nursing officer left to take up a new post, Ruth covered for her until the second left to have her baby. The four senior sisters were appointed to each of the ward areas, and the change was completed. However, Ruth realised that making the new jobs work properly would be a much longer process.

From her discussions, she knew that she would have to enhance the status and the group cohesion of the senior sisters. She anticipated that the doctors would find the presence of managers on the wards to be a mixed blessing. Ruth had worked out how she would respond to these potential problems if they occurred:

- She made sure that she was always available to the senior sisters especially to talk about clinical issues
- She cut all her lines of formal communication with the rest of the trained staff, which had the effect of enhancing the position of the senior sisters in the eyes of their colleagues
- She met the senior sisters as a group each week for two hours, when both managerial and clinical issues could be discussed
- She also encouraged them to use one another informally for support and advice

As she predicted, the doctors were ambivalent about the changes. In the absence of the nursing officers, the doctors were unable to exercise their influence by taking sides between the nursing staff. When faced with unacceptable decisions by the senior sisters, they challenged the authority of the sisters by coming directly to Ruth. Once the doctors were in her office Ruth would listen, accept they had a problem and refer them back to the senior sister, taking care to call her and explain what had transpired. After two months the doctors gradually stopped coming and the system began to settle down. The senior sisters needed far less of Ruth's attention and the problems they dealt with in their meetings became less clinical and operational and much more to do with longer term issues.

This change happened two years ago and, though Ruth continued to monitor the quality of both professional nursing practice and operational management, the changes were sufficiently successful to become part of the natural order of the hospital.

However, Ruth (now a sub unit general manager) has been recently talking to her unit general manager about her plans for better resource management systems and about better integration of acute and community services for children. She knows that both these issues will impact upon management structures at the operational level, and she has again been pondering over the changes that may be required and how they might be implemented.

12.5 Implications for managing change

We have already discovered that organisations can be seen as a volatile set of partisans, each actively pursuing interests which may or may not coincide with those of the manager. Moreover, we have seen that despite having sufficient managerial authority to change things 'as of right', in reality individuals or groups of partisans may have the power to frustrate the manager's intentions. We have developed a general view that a manager who attempts to implement change must think carefully about the network of partisans, interests and power that have produced the status quo. To change outcomes, the manager must develop tactics to alter either the number of partisans or the nature of their interests so that, one way or another, the balance of bargaining power shifts to favour the manager.

Sometimes health managers are a little uneasy about accepting this micro-political perspective. It seems almost profane to substitute the orthodox approaches which entail rationality, consensus and authority for a micro-political view involving instability, sectional interests, conflict and power. Also, the tactics that are drawn from this perspective seem unwholesome when compared with the behaviour required of the 'rational' manager. Perhaps one of the difficulties in effecting change is that we cling to the 'sacred' even when it does not help us achieve the changes we desire.

It is obvious that Ruth understood the change from a micro-political perspective. After she had established the general nature of the desired changes, she began 'mapping' the key partisans and the nature of their interests in maintaining the status quo. She also considered how they would see the advantages and disadvantages that would result from the change being introduced.

She also tried to think through the 'countermoves' each partisan might make as the implementation continued, and what possible response she might make. Developing an open-ended series of moves and countermoves seems to be a vital analytical stage of the change process. Only then can a manager be confident (but never certain!) that the change can be effected. Without this creative chess game, played with an almost infinite range of moves and countermoves, managers can devote a great deal of energy trying to implement a change which could have been deemed unimplementable.

Note too, how Ruth went through a process of 'reconciliation'. She changed her original intentions as she saw how people would react and reconciled her 'optimal' solution with the implementation difficulties. This balancing can be seen by some as weak management, as giving way, but from the bargaining perspective it is an ineluctable element of making changes happen.

Ruth also began the complex process of 'influencing' the way in which the partisans saw their own interests. She explained the advantages, emphasising different elements of the changes so as to appeal to each group. For example she emphasised the recruitment problem to the director of nursing services. She assuaged the fears of the designate senior sisters and, in a meeting with the doctors, was not above threatening (albeit in a veiled way) an even worse consequence were her plans not accepted. In this way, through a process of 'preparation', she gradually tried to ensure that most of the partisans felt they stood to gain from the changes to be made.

We must accept Ruth's luck in that, because of the approach she took, no group actually opposed her. It may not always be that way. Even with the most careful preparation, 'head on' conflicts may occur. In that event, the skilled manager must first decide if the battle is worth it, and then seek to build coalitions of interest around her or his point of view, trying to break the cohesion of the opposing group. 'Deals' may be made with the antagonists on some other issue unrelated to the one in question in some quid-pro-quo arrangements, which, though informal, are a vital part of the fabric of organisational life. Had Ruth needed to use it, the deal inferred about the medical students and the use of the vacated office would be a good example.

Ruth also paid careful attention to the 'follow through' since she realised that 'making changes happen' goes on after the change has happened! For example, Ruth anticipated that the doctors, having paid lip service to the ideas behind the change, might not help make it work and might even behave in such a way as to undermine it. In order to counteract this possibility, she made sure that she did everything she could to bolster the authority of the senior sisters.

She drew them close to her, getting them to see her as the principal managerial and clinical reference point rather than the consultants. She encouraged them to identify with each other as a group. She offered them open access on clinical issues. She enhanced their position by referring the doctors back to the senior sisters whenever she could.

Perhaps the real sting of the case is in the tail. Having successfully made a change happen, the circumstances change again! Resource management and service integration show that this particular round of change was not going to last forever. It brings us back to our start point; that engineering change is the very breath of management rather than being a particular subset of managerial activity that is only employed in exceptional circumstances. Good managers are therefore constantly negotiating and bargaining with a large number of partisans (both within and beyond the organisational boundary) as they seek to maximise their influence over a wide portfolio of issues.

12.6 Summary

There is a danger that when using a case study in this way it might be inferred that the behaviour of this particular manager would be appropriate in other settings. We would argue emphatically that the tactics of change are unique to every case. Tactics must be:

● Issue specific, in that different sets of partisans will have an interest in different issues
● Organisation specific, in that one cannot assume that the same pattern of partisans and interests will attend the same issue in different organisations
● Time specific, in that the pattern of bargaining relationships is

so volatile that the same or similar issues may never be dealt with in the same way twice
● Person specific, in that others will have different perceptions and hunches about the creative parts of the bargaining process, and also may find different negotiating behaviour more fruitful

In discussing the management of change, therefore, this chapter has not provided a check list of 'things you must do' in every situation. Instead, it suggests that once you have moved beyond orthodox thinking and take a more descriptive, micropolitical view of the dynamics of organisational life, then the tactics for successfully managing change become almost common sense.

Bibliography

S. Bacherach and E. J. Lawler, *Power and Politics in Organisations* (London: Jossey Bass, 1980).
R. Beckhard and T. Reuben, *Organisational Transitions* (Wokingham: Addison Wesley, 1987).
D. J. del Bueno and C. M. Freund, *Power and Politics in Nursing Administration, a Casebook* (particularly the chapter 'Swimming with Sharks') (Bethesda: US National Health Publications, 1986).
J. Pfeffer, *Power in Organisations* (London: Pitman, 1981).

Index